How to Make
Money
in Mail-Order

How to Make
Money
in Mail-Order

L. Perry Wilbur

John Wiley & Sons, Inc.
New York • Chichester • Brisbane • Toronto • Singapore

This publication is designed to provide accurate and authoritative information in regard to the subject matter covered. It is sold with the understanding
that the publisher is not engaged in rendering legal, accounting, or other pro
fessional service. If legal advice or other expert assistance is required, the services of a competent professional person should be sought. FROM A DECLA-
RATION OF PRINCIPLES JOINTLY ADOPTED BY A COMMITTEE OF THE
AMERICAN BAR ASSOCIATION AND A COMMITTEE OF PUBLISHERS.

Library of Congress Cataloging-in-Publication Data

Wilbur, L. Perry.
  How to make money in mail-order / L. Perry Wilbur.
     p.   cm.
  Includes bibliographical references.
  ISBN 0-471-51529-9.—ISBN 0-471-51532-9 (pbk.)
     1. Mail-order business—United States. I. Title.
HF5466.W55 1990
658.8'72—dc20   89-70536
                                                                    CIP

Printed in the United States of America

90 91 10 9 8 7 6 5 4 3 2 1

Preface

Making more money for yourself in mail-order is the name of the game. And getting your healthy share of this $117-billion-plus industry via your own growing, prospering mail-order company is what this book is all about. The mail-order boom is on, with no end in sight, and I see no reason why you can't play a larger part in it.

Ever wonder just what makes a mail-order company a superachiever? I wondered about this when doing my first book on mail-order, called *Money In Your Mailbox* (New York: John Wiley & Sons, 1985). What did the likes of Joe Karbo, the L. L. Bean Company, Sears Roebuck, and other stars of mail-order do to become such superstars in the industry? They all activated eight vital elements of success. You'll find each one discussed in this book.

Mail-order is a business of ideas, and you'll find hundreds of them—for products, services, novelty possibilities, and other items you may want to consider adding to your present line—in this book. As an example, what about adding a "New Age" mail-order business, as a sideline of your company? New Age items are hot sellers nowadays.

Above all, this book is designed to guide you in planning your company's growth and in focusing on a wider horizon of profits and success in your business. The material in the book should be of special help to mail-order company owners and operators and all others interested in the industry. It's geared to help you bring in more orders and inquiries from mail-order ads and direct mail.

Along with a variety of tested materials to help you do more effective classified, display, and direct-mail advertising, you'll also find success stories, catalog guidelines and examples, a self-scoring test of your ambition, products that give you the best shot for success, a close look at some money-making plans and programs currently being sold by mail, advice on getting repeat orders, mailing-list and direct-mail strategies, and more.

Specific steps for streamlining your offers and ad copy appeals so they'll bring in more orders and profits for your company are also outlined. There's material on finding the money to expand your business, with some addresses of people who may be able to help. The bonus and "P.S. double whammy" are discussed, along with a useful tip from billionaire Howard Hughes—something he accomplished that we can all learn from. Plans for achieving your mail-order goals also appear in this book, as do methods for maintaining a competitive edge.

I make eight important predictions concerning how the mail-order industry will look by the turn of the century. This information is bound to help you make more money and be more successful with your company now, in the year 2000, and well into the twenty-first century.

This book will make a very useful companion guide to my book *Money In Your Mailbox*. The book you are holding will lead your mail-order company to new vistas of success.

All the best to you. A world of super profits awaits you in the coming boom years in the mail-order business. Go for it! May your mailbox stay crammed with so many orders that you'll need a dozen more mailboxes to hold them all.

Contents

PART I

Today's Golden Opportunity in Mail-Order

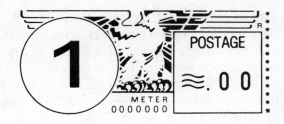

Cashing in on the Mail-Order Boom

Making your mark in mail-order via your own prosperous, growing company is what this book is all about. Often called the last frontier of fortune building, the fascinating mail-order business is a great place to be today, especially for those with an innovative, entrepreneurial spirit. You're lucky to be a part of it, and still luckier if you already have a company in place and are doing business. The 1990s hold much promise. Super profits are out there waiting for you in this $117-billion-plus industry. Go for it with gusto.

There's an old saying that "the world steps aside for the person who knows where he or she is going." It really does.

As you build your mail-order company in the months and years ahead, keep one thing in mind: your will to win prosperity and success in this industry and to become a mail-order champion. This will to win is one of the most valuable things to have going for you in mail-order. With a powerful will, you can and will make money in the industry, and you will climb the mail-order success ladder. With enough will, along with the right product or service plus some luck and good timing, you just might make mail-order sales history and achieve success beyond your wildest dreams.

Think about it. By the time you read these words in print, this $117 billion a year figure will be larger, and will continue to grow month after month. This $117 billion was the amount that changed hands in 1989 in both consumer and business purchases. So this means that the $117-billion record has already been broken.

Another word for this incredible growth of the mail-order industry is spelled b–o–o–m. You're clearly in a boom business with no end in sight to the profits to be made.

There are a number of reasons for this boom. Heading the list is the simple fact that an ever-growing number of consumers are fed up with a complete lack of service in stores these days. Drop in your local department store, or other store of your choice, and see how long it takes for someone to wait on you. How many times have you seen sales clerks doing their nails or chatting? I've seen a number of them talking on the phone to friends. They seem to resent having to wait on an actual customer. And how many times have you been unable to find a salesperson at all? Is there any wonder more and more thousands of consumers are switching to mail-order for their purchases?

Walk-in stores may be obsolete one day, with the vast majority of consumers buying nearly everything they need or want by mail. Impossible? Not at all. It can happen, and it very likely will happen, unless retail stores become more efficient and eliminate long customer waits and plain rudeness. It may already be too late, because once buyers experience the ease and convenience of mail-order buying, they prefer it. At that point, retail stores may have lost their customers.

The ongoing result of many retailers' don't-care, get-lost attitude is rising mail-order sales.

In addition to absent sales clerks, rudeness, long lines, and mis- or unmarked merchandise, finding a parking place is often a problem, especially on weekends and during holiday periods. Compare this hassle with buying by mail. You simply drop an order into the mail, then sit back and wait for delivery. No lines, no rude clerks, no search for a parking place. No hunting in cluttered store aisles for the items you want. No wonder there's a mail-order boom going on in the United States.

SIX WAYS YOU CAN PROSPER

There are six key areas, or ways, in which you can make money in the mail-order business. Let's take a look at each in turn. They are:

1. Classified ads
2. Space ads
3. Direct mail
4. Radio and television advertising
5. Using mail-order as a promotion method
6. Mail-order catalogs

Classified Ads

Even well-established mail-order companies continue to use classified ads to increase sales. When these ads contain the right words, and when they're placed in the leading mail-order publications, they usually pay for themselves and often bring in a tidy profit as well.

I still remember a classified ad I used to see in almost every magazine I picked up, and in quite a few newspapers too. From my early teen years on, almost every issue of these magazines ran this little ad. The headline was always the same: "How to Write Short Paragraphs for Money." The ad went on to offer, in a few words, a correspondence course in writing and selling short filler material. Benson Barrett was the owner of the company that ran the ad. I later discovered that this ad was largely responsible for Barrett's successful company and considerable profits.

Some real marketing logic lay behind the ad. The advertiser knew that most people reading his ad might not like to think about having to write lengthy, involved material before offering it for sale to markets, but writing *short paragraphs* and other brief filler material would be much easier.

In other words, those who saw Barrett's ad could see themselves turning out short paragraphs and selling them. The ad was *believable* and made buyers feel they could really do what the ad said: earn extra money by writing short fillers for all kinds of markets.

The result was one of the most successful classified ads of its generation. Even as a teen, I was sure that Benson Barrett was making good money from his little ad. He had to be, because the ad was everywhere. Few, if any, advertisers continue to run the same ad in the same publications month after month, unless the ad is paying its way and producing a profit.

Classified ads are the foundation, the bread and butter, and the security framework for many a mail-order company. If space ads and direct-mail fail or have disappointing results, remember that you can always fall back on your classified business. Quite a few mail-order companies choose classified ads over all the other possibilities; and you may well decide that classified advertising is where you belong exclusively, or at least that it should be one important area of your specialization.

Space Ads

A clever and appealing space ad in a recent issue of *The Wall Street Journal* caught my eye. It's a good example of how effective this type of ad can be.

Arranged in a column format (10 by 2 1/2 inches), the ad showed four button-down dress shirts in a row, with prices given at the side of each shirt. These were $19.50, $21.00, $31.50, and $22.50, respectively. The eye-catching, bold headline made the *money-savings* point clearly: "Our alternative to $30.00 Button-Down Shirts." The obvious savings for any potential customer was $7.50 to $10.50 on three choices of shirts. Huntington Clothiers of Columbus, Ohio, ran the ad. I'm sure this space ad will pull in many orders for them.

As you no doubt already know, the price of space ads is going up and up. So before putting your money into this type of ad, you should try to be as certain as possible that your space ads are going to produce worthy profits for you, above and beyond the ads' cost.

Some mail-order operators discover that they have a talent or flair for doing space ads. So this type of ad may well become a mainstay of their business. Others combine both classified and space ads.

Direct Mail

Sooner or later, experienced and growing mail-order operators give direct mail a go for the money. One of the fastest growing branches of the mail-order industry, direct mail can produce very profitable results. But getting hold of quality lists of known mail-order buyers for the product or service you're selling, as well as the patience to try different sales letters, are musts.

It also takes time to develop a strong direct-mail package consisting of the right sales letter, order form, circular, and return envelope. Each one is vitally important to the success of the package.

The beauty of direct mail is the fact that once you know you've got a winner (a strong letter and direct-mail package), you can roll out your offer to hundreds of thousands of list names. Some companies send out their direct mail to *millions* of potential buyers. The results can be incredible profits for those companies sharp enough to come up with the right mix and able to get out such large mailings to quality lists of prospect names.

If you haven't yet done much in direct mail, try continually to learn as much about it as your time allows. At some point in your business's future, you will want to give it a try and test an offer via this route.

Radio and Television Advertising

A number of mail-order companies report good results from radio and television advertising. Television advertising can be very expensive, but radio commercials, which are much cheaper, can bring you many orders. Some stations will even produce a taped commercial for you to use at certain designated times. Then they will send you all the orders they receive. Your total cost will depend on how many times your commercial is run per week.

Using Mail-Order as a Promotion Method

Another key way you can prosper in mail-order is to use it as a promotion method for your business. Commercial business writers, for example, who do all kinds of copywriting assignments for corporations and ad agencies, must constantly promote their services to keep landing new clients. One major way they keep their names in front of marketing executives is to send them sales letters and similar literature advertising the kinds of copy work they can do, their experience, fee schedule, order forms, and related materials.

Companies that offer consultant services, tax preparation assistance, investment seminars, psychic readings, real-estate training, and other services and pursuits send out all manner of promotional materials on a regular basis. They know that this use of mail-order can and will deliver new clients.

Mail-Order Catalogs

I well remember a time when, temporarily, the number of orders my company was receiving dropped considerably. Some poor-quality name lists were the cause of this problem. I needed to do something fast to put new life into my company. I came up with the idea of a mail-order catalog—but *my* version of one.

What I had in mind was not a regular, full-size, four-color catalog, which can be very expensive, but rather a ''mini'' catalog. As it turned out, it consisted of a single attractive listing of eight items I realized I could offer by mail. These eight products included information and booklets I developed, a do-it-yourself will form, and a music career guide. Up to this time,

I had been offering only two separate product items. But with my bright, two-color mini-catalog, as I called it, orders soon came streaming in and my sales rose once again.

Somewhere down the road, you may decide that you want a full-size catalog out there working for your business. But until you're financially established and have built your company to the point where you have numerous items selling consistently, stay away from trying a regular, full-size catalog. There is no reason, however, for not getting your feet wet and testing the catalog option in a "mini" way. This could mean a one-page listing of several items you offer, three or four pages of items, or even a small booklet of products or services for customers to choose from. Just remember to go slowly with the catalog idea at first. If a one- or two-page mini-catalog does well for you, then perhaps later you can try a ten-page booklet of offers, or something even larger.

The way to success via this route, as in all mail-order areas, is to move slowly, test regularly, and continue to learn and develop as a mail-order operator.

MAIL-ORDER GIVES YOU FULL CONTROL

As the head of your own mail-order company, your future growth and success are in your hands. You have full control. As the person in charge who makes all the key decisions, you wear many different hats. These hats, or functions, include the following:

Promoter
Planner
Innovator
Organizer
Advertiser
Prospector
Research Director
Creative Director
Manager
Administrator

As the person in full control of your company, you are certainly a manager. You practice a *hands-on* style of management. Your hand is in every phase of your business, and whether your company prospers or drops like a wounded duck depends on you and what you do to make your company grow and become more successful.

How well you manage all the aspects of your company will determine your degree of success in mail-order. In his interview of 25 chief executive officers of different major companies, author George A. Steiner identified 14 characteristics:

1. Leadership capability
2. Ability to communicate effectively
3. Global perspective
4. Profit consciousness
5. Thorough knowledge of the business
6. Strategic imagination
7. Sensitivity to external forces
8. Broad intellect
9. High moral standards
10. Familiarity with public affairs
11. Willingness to take responsibility for effective advocacy
12. Ability to balance interests of constituents
13. Ability to maintain poise under a bewildering variety of conditions
14. Administrative ability

As owner-operator of your mail-order company, you have clearly taken charge, taken the reins of full control of your business. You more than likely have a strong self-image, possess an ability to interact with customers (if mostly by mail), believe in taking risks, and are certainly a thinker as well as a doer.

Few, if any, mail-order operators are unwilling to take risks. Didn't you take a risk when you came into the industry and set up your mail-order company? Launching your first product item for sale was also a risk, as it will be with each new product you add to your company line.

Mail-order is a business that calls for important thinking as well as doing. You must think about what kinds of products or services mail-order customers will respond to. You must also think about, and originate, the strongest ads and direct-mail literature you can come up with to sell your products or services.

Entrepreneurship, by its very nature, means being willing to take risks—to think, originate, and then execute your conclusions and objectives.

Entrepreneur Portia Isaacson creates business enterprises from ideas. Her definition of an entrepreneur is "an opportunity-seeking mechanism." Risk is certainly implied in the word "opportunity." To advance your mail-order company in the months and years ahead will mean a certain amount of risk taking. But you have little choice. You must take those risks to have a chance to achieve more success.

In the words of James E. Burke, chairman of the board of Johnson and Johnson, "You have to take risks today. Business has become much more competitive on a world-wide basis. The answer to that challenge is no different than it's ever been: You've got to get better and better, and if you don't, you will be left behind."

Having full control of your company and its future means you've got to be willing to go for today's golden opportunities in mail-order. Fulfilling this objective means that you must take specific steps to get your company growing and to keep it growing. Some of these action steps include the following:

1. Carefully planning a mail-order strategy
2. Adequately testing different advertising copy ideas
3. Making the right decision as to the correct media to use (for example, not advertising in local newspapers when you should be in large national magazines)
4. Avoiding too many risky gambles on creative ideas
5. Using enough advertising on a consistent basis
6. Not using certain types of advertising, such as space ads and local television, that are too expensive
7. Establishing an adequate budget to run your business on
8. Conducting a thorough study of the market you wish to reach with your mail-order product or service

MAIL-ORDER LETS YOU GRAB CUSTOMERS AT THEIR HOMES AND OFFICES

Those television sets sitting in most homes around the world are the means by which many major advertisers sell their goods and products to consumers. An endless stream of sales pitches and commercials flows from these tubes seven days a week. Like the frantic news anchorman in the hit film *Network*, the tube tells countless millions how to dress, what to eat, where to travel, and a host of other directives.

Your direct-mail literature may not have the magnetic appeal of television, but it does *arrive* in the office, home, or apartment of the prospective customer and has a better-than-average chance of being opened and looked at, if only briefly. If it's effective, grabs the person's attention, and arouses interest, it can lead to a sale and return order. Even your classified or space ads can reach out to potential customers provided they turn to the pages on which your ads appear and are drawn to *your* ads rather than the others.

This, then, is the challenge—to come up with ads and direct-mail sales letters that grab customers on the spot, whether they're in their offices or relaxing at home. To meet this challenge and build a successful, profitable company, there are facts you need to be aware of. At the top of the list is information regarding today's changing marketplace. Some major trends are now very clear:

- Women are entering the work force in growing numbers.
- Households are becoming smaller.
- Consumers are becoming more unique. They can't be as easily grouped, or lumped together, as in the past.
- Most families are now two-income families. Women now bring in 40 percent of the family income, and this will very likely increase.
- Consumer attitudes are changing along with living arrangements and the family structure itself.
- An "affluent society" is emerging.
- Consumers are looking for products and services that offer more *value* for their dollars.

All the changes above, and others, affect the many decisions made by consumers:

- How they work
- How they think
- Where they live
- What they buy
- What they read
- How they relax and play
- How they keep warm and cool

A GREAT PLACE FOR YOUR CREATIVE IMAGINATION

Mail-order, over the next ten years and beyond, will be a great place for you to use your creative imagination.

You have *freedom* in mail-order to copy existing products and services, by which I mean you can sell the same types of products, or ones very similar to those offered by others. You can change or improve existing products, or create new products and services and market them.

This freedom in the industry to offer similar products or to blaze new trails is part and parcel of the golden opportunity that is today's mail-order industry.

In *The Uncommon Man in American Business*, author Wallace Johnson highlights a significant point: "Too many people are thinking of security instead of opportunity. They seem more afraid of life than of death."

Author Dean Alfange states his case for opportunity: "I seek opportunity . . . not security. I want to take the calculated risk, to dream and to build, to fail and to succeed."

Your creative imagination can be the fuel that pushes you and your company into ever higher realms of profit and success. I'm talking about creative imagination applied to (1) changes and additions to existing products and services; (2) brand-new product items; (3) classified, space ads, and direct-mail packages; (4) list strategies; (5) testing; (6) finding seed money and capital to build your business; and (7) maintaining a competitive edge.

Do you ever wonder who was the most creative human being? Many people maintain that the greatest creative genius in recorded history was Leonardo da Vinci. Leonardo was an innovator, and as owner-operator of your own mail-order company, you're an innovator, too.

Innovation is work. It requires knowledge, imagination, and originality. Ingenuity helps a lot, too. Peter Drucker, in *Imagination and Entrepreneurship*, states that innovation "is an effect in economy and society. Innovation always has to be close to the market, focused on the market, and market driven."

Direct-mail sales letters and full-page ads offer *tremendous* opportunities for applying your creative imagination. On a smaller scale, so do classified ads.

More effective use of creative imagination can do the following for your company:

1. Produce attention-riveting headlines for your ads
2. Streamline the body copy of your ads
3. Originate exciting new product and service ideas
4. Produce result-getting promotional methods for an existing business
5. Suggest ways to help your company grow and prosper

A strong example of effective creative imagination can be seen in this ad headline from the *San Francisco Shopper*. The ad is for binoculars:

You can look the sparrow
straight in the eye from
250 feet and you can see it
blink.

Now there's a specific, positive, interest-grabbing headline, and it cuts through skepticism like tissue paper. It shows good use of creative imagination.

THE IDEAL WAY TO START OR EXPAND A BUSINESS

The asking price for start-up business franchises these days runs from about $20,000 to $200,000 or more. A McDonald's franchise, at last report, cost a whopping $500,000. How many people interested in having their own business can come up with the six figures necessary to buy that franchise? Not many.

This is one of the most attractive features about starting a mail-order company of your own. The start-up costs are very reasonable. Just a few years back, you could launch a mail-order company with as little as a few hundred dollars. Today it takes at least $500—many would say $1,000 or more. But that amount is trivial compared with the franchise fees asked by established, ''name'' companies.

Mail-order operators have another choice available to them in that they can run their companies on either a full-time or part-time basis. Many businesses require full-time, 40-hour (or more) workweeks. But in mail-order, you can choose to start slowly if you wish and run your company as a sideline business. Many of today's established and successful mail-order companies began as sideline pursuits run on the weekends and perhaps a few hours several nights a week.

This direct chance to start slowly while learning more about mail-order as you grow brings many newcomers into the industry year after year.

Running your company as a sideline venture gives you time to discover what you like and dislike about the business, what skills and abilities are most helpful, what product items and services seem to do well in the marketplace, and what your own goals for the future of your company might be.

In other words, starting and operating on a part-time basis allows you time to analyze the nature of the business before going full time—while actually being in it. That's a definite advantage for you.

Anthony J. F. O'Reilly, currently chief executive officer of the H. J. Heinz Company, believes that considering a situation carefully before moving on it is wise: ''I like to analyze a situation very thoroughly before I make my move. As a football player that is one thing I did: I always hung back. While this has surely caused me to miss some opportunities, I have made very few major mistakes. By taking this approach, I think that I have kept the mistake factor at a tolerable level and have made a few touchdowns as well.''

Mail-order also can quickly come to the aid of those business owners who seek to expand their sales, profits, and overall growth. How does mail-order help them accomplish these results? By selling their products or services *via the mail*. Remember, almost anything can be sold by mail, though obviously many items are more suitable for mail-order than others. Many a company owes its increased profits and expansion to the simple fact that it added a mail-order wing to its operation and advertised in the right places for a long enough time or put together an effective direct-mail package.

THE CATALOG OPTION: A WIN-WIN SITUATION

The dream of many mail-order operators is to have their own multi-color, full-length catalog out there in the homes and offices of millions of customers and prospective customers. It's a worthy objective, but you must realize up front that full-size catalogs are obviously expensive to produce and distribute. They require a great deal of sound judgment, careful product planning and selection, coordination, and follow-through.

One very active catalog producer is United States Purchasing Exchange, or USPE. In business for 35 years, this is no small-potatoes operation. USPE produces and distributes seven or more catalogs a year, with the Christmas and summer catalogs being the leaders. As USPE states in its literature, ''Not every customer on our mailing list is selected to receive all our mailings. Additional selections are made for bonus items and sweepstakes entries.''

Along with giving each of its catalogs an attractive, eye-catching cover, USPE makes very effective use of color pictures of all items offered in its catalogs. The old cliché ''one picture is worth a thousand words'' still holds true today. As you would expect, these sharp, multicolor pictures of products, often shown *in actual use* by buyer-customers, do a great deal to entice potential buyers.

What are some of the products offered in the USPE catalog? The spring catalog offers a variety of car accessories, shoes, handbags, kitchen towels, wallets, cameras, tables, lamps, items for the yard, fitness machines, digital pedometers, dresses, robes, underwear, pillows, coin collections, cutlery sets, socks, bedspreads, linen and lace tablecloths, pantyhose, paint sprayers, radios, bath scales, flashlights, toys, floor fans, bug repellers, knife sharpeners, can openers, and many other items. In other words, anything and everything to make a person's life easier, more comfortable, more convenient, safer, pleasanter, and more entertaining, especially during the spring season.

Prices in the spring 1989 catalog ranged from about $7.97 for a pair of handsome moccasin slippers to $99.97 for a complete AM/FM dual cassette stereo system. The point is that this, and every, USPE catalog offers items to fit any budget.

I've ordered quite a few items from a number of USPE catalogs, and I've always been very pleased with the products. USPE delivers promptly (even during holiday periods), and customers rarely have to wait very long to receive the items they order.

THE RULES OF DIRECT MAIL APPLY TO CATALOGS

Obviously, many of the basic rules of direct mail also hold true for a catalog. These include the following:

- Strong use of illustrations, preferably showing items in actual use
- Effective layout and design
- A full description of each product offered
- "Magnetic" pictures that lead prospective customers to read the copy that goes with each pictured item
- The use of comparisons and testimonials in the copy

The Catalog's Main Objective

The number one goal of a catalog is to get orders, to lead customers and prospects to *take action* by buying direct from the catalog.

Every catalog page must pull its own weight. It must show the items in an attractive way. The copy has to be sharp, crisp, captivating, and supported by strong headlines.

Often, a mail-order company will test specific pages, items, or places in a catalog to see what the results will be. Occassionally, an item may be offered twice in the same catalog issue. This technique usually increases sales.

Some catalog companies fail to make strong enough use of covers. Catalogs are being distributed with weak, ineffective covers. In contrast, *Entrepreneur* magazine recently distributed a catalog of business guides with an excellent cover. The title—''The Be-Your-Own-Boss Catalog''—was intriguing, and the subtitle said it all: ''227 ways to succeed in a business of your own.'' Beneath the title and subtitle, a series of four-color pictures showed men and women in action scenes running their businesses. The businesses described in this appealing, 48-page catalog included the following:

A ''sweats-only'' store
A children's bookstore
A diner
A convenience food store
A coffee shop
A seminar-promotion guide
A video store
A pest-control business
A limousine service
A deli sandwich shop
A sporting goods store
An earring shop
A cosmetics shop
A non-alcoholic bar
A cookie shop
A burglar-alarm business
An ad agency

The average price for these business guides was $69.50, but regular subscribers to *Entrepreneur* were offered the guides for $59.50. This is an example of an effective catalog, with every page advertising six or seven business guides, and the front and back covers grabbing the attention of prospects. The back cover again gave the title of the catalog, showed two businesses being operated by owners, and also included recommendations of the catalog by major newspapers such as the *Los Angeles Herald Examiner* and the *Arizona Republic*.

As you plan and build your mail-order company in the coming years, try in your free time to learn all you can about catalogs. Many mail-order operators aim for a catalog as their eventual target. But remember that it takes money, time, and top planning to produce a quality catalog, not to mention the need for a four-star line of products. But once you do get a good, well-distributed catalog out there, you can make a great deal of money, and I mean *profits* over expenses.

One of the best things a catalog has going for it, and keep this in mind, is the fact that customers often keep catalogs for long periods of time, delaying their buying decisions. Then, wham, one day they pick up the catalog, thumb through it, and decide to send in one order . . . or a flock of orders.

In other words, a well-produced catalog has *staying power*. It can bring in orders and profits for you over a long period of time.

Until you're well established in the industry and have developed enough items to begin thinking about a catalog, I suggest you delay doing one. But you can definitely plan on it as a target goal; and I certainly urge you to try your wings with a mini-catalog, as described earlier. A mini-catalog lets you get your feet wet, learn about catalogs in a very limited way, and experiment without sinking a lot of money and time into the operation. But even a mini-catalog requires that you have at least several product items (or services) to offer prospects and customers.

As your mail-order company grows and you add new products or services to your line, the day may come when it's time to think about a full catalog. If and when you reach that point, you'll be standing at the brink of what may prove to be another catalog success story. You will have then attained one of the ultimate goals and satisfactions in mail-order—a color catalog of your own with your company name on it. If and when you get that chance, by all means go for it. Just proceed with caution and common sense, as well as optimism and excitement. Even your first full catalog may prove to be the foundation for your success and mail-order fortune.

Mail-Order Is a Business of Ideas

If you're fortunate enough to be an "idea person," you should do well in mail-order sooner or later. Mail-order is a business of ideas. In his book *Self-Consciousness*, author John Updike makes an interesting statement about work: "Work is the only practical consolation for having been born." In his own life, Updike feels that his productivity has been his salvation.

Idea tracking in mail-order does not seem like work, at least to a great many mail-order operators. The ideas that kick around in a mail-order person's head are fascinating, appealing, and magnetic gems that may come to the person at any time—in the shower, on the way to work, during sleep, watching a ballgame on television, or whenever.

Though some products and services are similar and may overlap, many are fresh, different, and possibly even unique, at least in their early stages.

You may well get an idea for a mail-order product that is already being sold successfully by other companies. This does not mean you can't offer the same item and make money doing it. Your product or service may be very similar to others that already exist, but if other mail-order companies are doing well with items similar to yours, that is a good sign you will succeed, too.

SEE WHAT OTHER COMPANIES ARE OFFERING

As a veteran in the industry, you're probably aware of one excellent idea-stimulator for possible new products. Order some of the items currently being offered by other companies. The small cost to you is well worth the chance to see what competing mail-order companies are selling. If these other companies are continuously running ads or sending out direct mail, then they must be doing well and making a profit.

When you receive an item, look it over to see if there's some change, improvement, or addition you could make in the existing product. In mail-order, every idea doesn't have to be for a completely new product or service. You can adapt, change, add to, or slightly alter existing product items and perhaps do very well for yourself. In other words, you can originate in two ways: by originating with a brand new product or by applying some original thinking to existing products and services to see what you come up with. This just might develop into a profitable new item for you that will bring in orders.

Don't be misled if some of the ideas you come up with seem overly simple. The amazing *paperclip* certainly sounded simple, and it was. But look at what a marvelous role it has played in the lives of so many millions over many years. The humble paperclip has long been considered one of the most useful products of the modern era. It made its creator a huge fortune. And what keeps the money rolling in is the fact that the paperclip is a *repeat* product. Consumers keep coming back and buying more and more clips.

Keep in mind also that some of the most wonderful ideas for new products, inventions, businesses, and services have *yet to be* originated. There are always fresh angles for a new business cooking in somebody's mind.

Businessman Carl Carson rented cars and trucks for most of

his career. Then he went into the rent-an-executive business, with himself as the executive-for-rent. ''My experience is in the area of marketing,'' he says. ''I approach small businesses that do not have the need for a $150,000 marketing executive. I sell them my time for one day, a week, or a month. I use my 58 years of marketing experience.''

PICK MAIL-ORDER ITEMS WITH ORIGINALITY AND FLAIR

While many mail-order companies have found success by copying the successful products and services of established firms, someone with originality and a flair for picking sound mail-order items can do especially well. Quite a variety of items are purchased by mail these days. A recent check of just a few items being offered via mail-order turned up the following:

- Newsletters
- Investment advice
- Divorce kits
- Old records
- Tape cassettes
- Speed-reading courses
- Will and test forms
- Handwriting analysis
- Lottery numbers
- Menu services
- Mailbox covers
- Pipe stands
- Boots
- All manner of books and booklets
- Various baby items

WHAT DOES IT MEAN TO ORIGINATE?

I think of it as the willingness, desire, and interest to try something new. Everyone has the potential for being able to originate, to think up something fresh and original. Walt Disney dreamed of an amusement park for children built around his cartoon and film characters. Disneyland and Disney World were the happy results.

THE PROFIT IN ORIGINAL IDEAS CAN BE STAGGERING

Whoever came up with the idea of advertising soft drinks as "caffeine free" probably picked up a hefty bonus at the very least.

Jim Fixx, author of *The Complete Book of Running*, couldn't believe the amount on his first royalty check for that book. It was for $750,000. He took the check to his bank, not believing they would accept it. They did. He had thought the book might sell 30,000 copies. Instead, it sold millions. Of course the book's timing was ideal. The jogging craze was then sweeping the United States, and this naturally gave his book an enormous boost.

These are of course "super" examples. There are many other more ordinary cases where the originator added many hundreds or many thousands of dollars to his or her bank account, by offering a product for home improvement, by solving a business problem, by designing attractive new clothes, by inventing a new toy or game, or whatever.

THE IMPORTANT ROLE OF CURIOSITY IN ORIGINALITY

The curiosity of the innovator, or originator, is what often leads the person to experiment to try to create something new. This curiosity may well take the form of such questions as these:

- How can I change an existing product?
- Can it be modernized?
- Can it be made smaller or larger?
- Can it be made more appealing, colorful, enjoyable, or easier to handle?

SUCCESS STORY: John Bear

John Bear got into the mail-order business with a good idea: He decided to publish and advertise a report on how to get a college degree by mail. One of John's early ads cost him $120 and returned a gross of $7,000. His net profit turned out to be about $5,000.

Delighted with his success in mail-order, Bear made some changes in his life. He left his job in Chicago and moved to northern California. Reportedly, he now runs his ad in more than 30 leading mail-order publications and enjoys a handsome retirement income from his considerable profits.

While some people in and out of mail-order overestimate their talent and originality, many others underestimate themselves, get into the wrong pursuits, or take a detour from the work they ought to be doing. Every person has at least *some* talents and natural abilities. More emphasis should be placed on finding and developing them.

"THE LAZY MAN'S WAY TO RICHES"

When they write the history of super-successful mail-order sellers, the name of Joe Karbo will no doubt be near the top of the heap. If you've been in mail-order for a reasonable period of time, it's very likely you've seen the Karbo name and read about his enormous success with his classic book, *The Lazy Man's Way to Riches*.

Joe Karbo's corporation rose to the coveted position of handling more than *two million* dollars worth of business transactions a year. Now that's mail-order success.

How did Joe do it? He sold a six-by-nine-inch paperback book of 156 pages at $10.00 per copy. To sell his book, Joe used a series of full-page ads in leading national mail-order magazines. He sold more than 600,000 copies of his book, but his *product* wasn't really the book at all, but rather the *information* he provided. The many thousands who bought the book from Joe wanted in on his secrets of how to make a lot of money the easy, lazy-person's way.

An incredible thing about Karbo's success was the fact that he started advertising his book before it was even written. He ran his ad copy and quickly discovered he had a huge winner on his hands. As I've said a number of times already, and as I'll continue to say throughout this book, Joe Karbo *tested* first. He had no idea if his product would be a bomb or not. So he tested the concept, the advertising copy for the product, to see what would happen. He was overwhelmed with the response and promptly got the book written, printed, and ready to be sent to the thousands of buyers who wanted it.

NOVELTY ITEMS CAN BE SUPER-SELLERS

One man in Pennsylvania has made over a million dollars selling mail-order novelty items. Novelty items currently being offered through mail-order include talking balloons; a bell that alerts parents when a baby's diapers need to be changed; T-shirts with special punch lines, designs, slogans, or catchphrases on them; illustrated business cards; ''appreciation gift'' items for business owners or salespeople (such as pen sets and key hooks); ''snore-no-more'' arm sensors; unusual or extra-powerful flashlights; unusual dolls; and many other novelty items.

Not very long after the death of Elvis Presley, one enterprising mail-order operator came up with the idea of offering Elvis Presley wallpaper showing scenes from the legendary singer's life and career. Sales were very strong for a good period of time.

The *timing* of a novelty item can often be a very important factor in its success or failure. The Elvis wallpaper naturally sold well in the period following the singer's death. Anything and everything about Elvis, or with his name and picture on it, sold like hotcakes because of the shock his death caused and the demand it created.

Novelty items offer one of the best product categories in mail-order for exercising your creative imagination. Here are some suggestions to help you come up with strong new novelty items. Who knows? Any one of your ideas, or a combination of several, might make you a fortune. Follow these question guidelines:

1. Is your novelty idea fresh and different?
2. Is there a large market of mail-order customers-prospects for it?
3. Is it something that would have built-in repeat sales? (Your real profits could come from any repeat sales of the item.)
4. Can you produce it cheaply enough and sell it at a high enough price to make a good profit?
5. Is it something that would add quality and profit to your present line of products or offers?

"$25,000 PER WEEKEND"

Since mail-order is a business of ideas, it's not surprising that all kinds of money-making plans and programs are offered by mail-order companies. Most people out there want more money. The actual spending value of today's dollar is about 30 cents—some say only a thin quarter. It takes close to a thousand dollars today to do what a hundred used to. Just a pack of chewing gum nowadays sells for 90 cents or more in many airports. That's almost 20 times as much as it was back in the 1950s.

So the large majority of people, including those who buy by mail regularly, want and need more money. With this great need in mind, a number of mail-order companies have come up with all manner of money-generating programs, plans, systems, and businesses. What they are pitching to prospects are methods of producing cash money—and plenty of it.

I've ordered many of these products and money plans myself in order to study and compare them. Almost every one of them turns out to be a booklet, usually very thin and cheaply produced. Only the minimum number of pages needed is used to tell how the plan works. Some of these plans are easily explained in as few as 20 pages.

By way of example, one of these, titled *$25,000 Per Weekend*, is only 23 pages long, yet its price is $15.00 plus $2.00 more for postage and handling. This particular plan involves holding beauty pageants. The booklet claims that the buyer of the plan can make $25,000 in a single weekend. The money is generated through fees of $600 paid by individual or business sponsors.

While this plan reads like it could work, I wonder how many who have tried it have actually made $25,000 or even half that amount in a weekend. Still, it must have sold many copies because I saw the ad for it quite a few times in different magazine issues.

The strongest thing this plan has going for it, as is the case for most other money-making programs, is the ad that is used. The ad grabs attention and convinces prospects to send in orders.

Let's examine some of the key ingredients of the ad for this booklet product:

Headline: $25,000 Plus Every Weekend

Subhead: This First Time Ever Revealed Secret Program Will Allow Anyone to Earn Huge Amounts of Money Every Weekend without Startup Costs!

First line pitch: The information you are now reading will change your life.

Colors used: Green and black in this ad

Guarantee: 200 percent money-back guarantee

How many go ahead and actually hold a beauty contest (after ordering the program) is anyone's guess. The point is that it continues to sell well at the time I'm writing. I have seen the two color, full-page ad for this product in a number of opportunity magazines. It must be bringing in lots of orders, or the company wouldn't continue to run it. How much longer it will pull in orders is anybody's guess, but I would say that the ad has done well.

You must understand an important truth about these money-making plans and programs. Far more people order them than actually try to put them into action. For some reason, often plain curiosity, many will buy such a plan but then never try to follow the scheme it proposes. They just read the booklet and then forget all about it. A great many buyers are *disappointed* when they receive these items, and the reason for that is clear. The ads used to sell many of these plans are almost always much better and appealing than the products themselves.

In fact, it's a standard rule in mail-order that a top-notch ad can sell a poor, or low-quality, product. The ad is where the focus is. A mail-order operator might have the greatest product in the world, but if the ad used to sell it is poor and doesn't grab attention, there's very little chance for success.

Clearly, you've got to have a terrific ad and, preferably, a quality product. Unfortunately, a number of products on the market are not as good as the ads for them. It took me some time to learn this, but it becomes very apparent once you order some of these plans and compare the items you ordered with the ads that sold them. In just about every case, the quality of the ad is head and shoulders above the product.

"GOVERNMENT LOOPHOLES"

I responded to an ad selling a money-making scheme based on "government loopholes," but I never received what was advertised. (This wasn't the first time that has happened!) I wrote several times and telephoned the magazine in which the ad appeared. It did no good. My $12.00 plus $2.00 more for first-class postage, a total of $14.00, was a complete loss.

Here are the ingredients of the ad:

Headline: Little Known Government Loophole and My Never Before Revealed System Will Make You a Millionaire in the Next 60 Days

Subhead: It's perfect! The first 100% fail-proof money-making idea. No one who has tried it has failed.

First line pitch: For the first time ever, you can be assured success.

Colors used: Black headline and red subhead

Guarantee: $100 if buyer uses the program and fails

Do you notice the similarities with the first ad? The chance to make big money is the bait, and the potential customer is even assured of success in the first sentence. Almost all of these ads make it sound as if they offer money in the bank.

In this case, chances are that the ad did well for the advertiser. The full-page ad was repeated in consecutive monthly issues of the magazine. With the cost of full-page magazine advertising today, no mail-order advertiser would continue to repeat a large ad unless it pulled in orders and was profitable.

"THE ONLY WAY TO COMPLETE PROSPERITY"

Another variation on the idea of a money-making plan sold via mail-order is the use of a religious approach. I ordered a booklet recently that advocates the practice of tithing, that is, giving up to 10 percent of your income, in expectation of receiving a *larger* return.

There are some books and booklets like this on the market, though not many. The whole idea of the one I bought is that God wants us (from the ad I assume most of us) to be wealthy and prosperous. As the booklet says, "God rules the world and He wants to make us wealthy if we follow His guidelines defined in the holy Bible." A dozen Bible verses were quoted in the booklet to support this premise.

Almost halfway through the 20-page booklet, "three steps for riches" are presented. They are (1) "God is your source," (2) "Give and it will be given you," and (3) "Expect a miracle."

Finally, the reader-buyer is challenged to test God by actually tithing whatever amount he or she can manage up to a full 10 percent. The booklet ends with some bonus material on how to pray for special results.

This booklet-product must have done well for its advertiser, because the full-page magazine ad I saw for it cost plenty to run month after month. On the other hand, it might have been a test and only advertised in several issues. I haven't seen the ad anywhere else lately.

This ad's headline was a strong one:

Headline: Finally! The Most Powerful Millionaire-Maker in History

NEW PRODUCTS AND BUSINESS IDEAS BY ACCIDENT

It's very important that you be aware of the fact that entrepreneurial types, like yourself, sometimes stumble upon very good, new business ideas. An entrepreneur or an inventor may be working on something quite different, or looking for other information, when, wham, a bright, fresh, and possibly terrific product discovery or business idea is made and realized.

Educators and experts who study innovation say that the usual pattern for these new discoveries is an accidental one. So stay on your entrepreneurial toes. Keep your eyes, ears, and mind open and alert. Just one terrific new product or business idea discovery could skyrocket your company's mail-order profits. Go for it!

MULTI-LEVEL AND NETWORK MARKETING PLANS

Today's high technology companies are having trouble coming up with strong new products. Quite a few companies are still relying on their old products to earn most of their profits.

In mail-order, a new way of doing business has been emerging during the last decade. The labels used to describe this are "multi-level marketing" and "network marketing."

Knowing that I might one day be writing about multi-level and network marketing, I tried my hand at each method at two separate companies. I worked in my spare time to make a go of each. In one company, all members were required to purchase a monthly amount of product. I bought the monthly amount for awhile, although I did not consume it. The product was health foods, in this case. There were people in the company, however, that not only loved the health foods product; they also were able to sign up many others to be distributors, like themselves, and therefore received a rising amount of money based on their own sales plus what the distributors they brought in could do.

The point is clear. Some people in multi-level and network marketing programs are doing well. They seem to have a knack for these ways of doing business. But many others only make a fair return. Although some of these programs don't make it clear that personal selling is involved, the ability to convince others to sign up is crucial for real success. If you can sell on a face-to-face basis and are comfortable with it, you might do very well with a multi-level or network marketing program.

Those people you sign will, in turn, get others to join, and this multi-level structure can build a big income for you. Some multi-level companies state in their literature that ''one out of every five millionaires made their fortune in multi-level or network-marketing companies.'' What you can earn can vary from a few hundred to a few thousand, or up to $10,000 or more per month. This lucrative potential is what draws many newcomers to try their hand at this way of doing business. Some have reportedly become millionaires in such programs.

Multi-level and network marketing are not for everyone. Before you make any commitment along these lines, study well the company programs that you're considering. One thing is for sure: A number of persons are doing amazingly well in these ''new'' areas of marketing. (That is, they're new to most of the public. Actually, such programs have been around for years.)

PSYCHIC CONSULTING BY MAIL

Watch your mail this week because there's a strong chance you'll hear from one or more ''psychic consultants.'' These people, who claim to be able to glimpse the future, are pitching their service to you (and many more prospects) by mail.

Recently direct-mail sales letters from these psychics have definitely increased. I know I hear from more of them than I used to. They've got my name on their lists.

One key idea many of these psychics are selling is that, for a fee (usually $15.00 to $20.00 at this writing), they will send you the exact six numbers you should play to win the lottery. Their literature makes it sound like you're practically a shoo-in to win one or more big cash jackpots.

Quite a few of these psychics run classified ads in leading tabloid newspapers as well as in various magazines. The service they pitch lends itself well to direct mail, classified ads, and even space ads in certain selected publications. If you have any interest in this area, you might do well. These psychics would not keep sending their sales letters out and running classified ads unless orders were flowing back to them.

Naturally, it would be a great plus if you *really* did have psychic talent and ability. I often wonder, after reading some of their sales letters, if any of them know any more about the future, or which six lottery numbers are best, than I do.

If you are psychic or believe you could help people with their lives and problems—whether that means winning a lottery, solving marital problems, getting stock market help, or whatever—you might consider this idea for a mail-order business. The ability to promote your psychic consultant service by mail and to develop believable literature (sales letters) would be important for your success.

I used to know a college professor in Kentucky who, at the time, was making more money through his astrological chart service, both for local people and for out-of-towners via mail-order, than he did as a professor. Back then, he charged $250 to $300 for a chart; no doubt that fee would be much higher today. His ability to work up complete astrological charts paid off handsomely for him.

Mail-order companies and operators should keep this type of service in mind. There's money to be made in the stars and the occult. A lot of these services, and the books, materials, and booklets that go with them, have been lumped into the category of "New Age." Maybe a New Age mail-order business would send you to your bank frequently with handsome profits to deposit in your company name. As some authorities on this subject say, "Everyone is psychic to one degree or another."

Perfect Home-Based Money-Making Businesses

From my own experience, observation, study, and interviews with other mail-order operators, I find that some of the most successful home-based, money-making businesses are those that offer booklets and pamphlets on increasing the buyer's income or starting a business.

What prospective buyer or already-existing customer wouldn't like to increase his or her monthly and yearly income? Many of these prospects may not like the books available to them in regular bookstores or department stores. In fact, the book sections of many department stores are pretty skimpy these days. Often, the most helpful books are sold only via mail-order and cannot be found in stores anywhere.

As an example, I recently received in the mail a black-and-white, four-page brochure, order form, and return envelope for a product headlined ''The Incredible $1 Million Secret!'' Odds are very high that this product is a pamphlet or booklet describing some method for earning money.

Like most others, this particular booklet-product probably gives advice on how to succeed in one of the following areas:

Real estate
Stock investing
Import-export
Money brokering
Business consulting
Self-publishing
Mail-order plans
Lottery systems
Distributor programs
Network marketing
Multi-level plans
Pyramid schemes (Pyramids, by the way, are illegal.)
Various other start-up businesses

A "perfect" home-based money-making business usually offers some type of printed information that, when put into action, promises to bring in a cash flow and increase the buyer's monthly income.

For the last decade, there has been an explosive demand for information of all sorts. The mail-order industry has met this huge demand head-on and has offered a wide variety of money-making businesses that customers can launch without spending a fortune. This selling of information has to be one of the major product areas of the industry. Information has become king, and it will remain that way through the 1990s and possibly well into the next century.

I hope you realize what this can mean for you. Even if you already sell some type of information by mail, you may not have scratched the surface. Many mail-order operators are adding new information products to their existing lines on a regular basis. You may be able to do the same. Quite a few mail-order companies specialize in information, and you may decide to focus on this area yourself. Thin pamphlets sell. Booklets often do nicely. And many full-length books sell far better, and for a much longer time, by mail-order than they would if sold in traditional bookstores or department stores.

It's the particular kind of information being offered that makes a product sell. It's not the cover, illustrations (if any), or thickness (or thinness) of the pamphlet or booklet. What your prospects and buyers want and care about is the information inside. Can it help them make more money? Does it tell them how to start and run a business? Will the information presented help the buyer to enrich his or her life? If so, then you've probably got a winner.

STAPLE ITEMS PEOPLE AND BUSINESSES NEED

Quite a few mail-order companies have done well by offering staple items needed by businesses and individuals alike. Such items include the following:

1. Rubber stamps
2. Printing and office supplies
3. Mailing lists (names and addresses of prospects)
4. Home-study courses
5. Security items (for instance, self-defense or karate instructions)
6. Resume service (for individuals searching for jobs)
7. Income tax help
8. Computer accessories
9. Consultant services
10. Advertising services (needed by companies more than by individuals)

A good example of staple items that both individual people and businesses need would be printing and office supplies. As long as individuals and companies stay in business, they have a need for professional-looking letterhead stationery, business and return envelopes, circulars, sales letters, order forms, invoices, carbon paper, and so on down a fairly long list.

The big plus of selling staple items like these is the fact that many customers will continue to send you repeat orders as long as the quality of your products stays high, the prices are fair, and you consistently deliver orders promptly.

THE LURE OF WEALTH, SECURITY, AND FREEDOM

If any of the items you presently sell by mail offer the promise of wealth-building, security, and financial freedom, these products may well become the strongest, most profitable, and most consistent sellers in your line. If you're not offering any items that help customers increase their incomes, perhaps you can originate one or more.

A short while ago, I received via direct mail one of the most magnetic sales letters I've ever seen, and I've read and studied thousands of them over the years. This one truly impressed me. My first thought on opening the envelope, as a great many recipients of sales pitches must also think, was "Here it comes." Here comes another sales talk for something I don't want, need, or even care about.

But guess what happened? The excellent letter hooked me. The letter's lure was one of the most powerful I've ever experienced. The specific lure was financial independence. The letter's four pages held my attention from start to finish. The clincher was an additional, one-and-a-half-page guarantee. The guarantee had this eye-catching headline: "Exclusive 'No Risk' 5 Year/$5,000 Guarantee!"

Now that's a very strong guarantee, and it did a lot to convince me to send in my order. I know of no other mail-order offer, at least at the present time, that offers such a powerful guarantee.

The section headings of the letter were also equally strong. One of them, for example, read like this: "The Amazing Thing Is the Speed at Which This System Works!"

The body copy of the letter inspired my belief and trust in the seller-sender of this product, which was an information package. After reading the letter twice, and the guarantee page as well, I simply knew I wanted to order. To tell you the truth, I felt compelled to order. And that's what I did.

Please bear in mind that the bait for these wealth-building programs and plans is the promise they make. The only way a prospect can discover if the plan will really do what it's cracked up to do is to order it, try it, and see firsthand.

Millions of people everywhere are looking for plans, pro-

THE ENTREPRENEUR'S SPIRIT

Jean Taylor, president of Archives, Incorporated, which rents atmosphere-controlled storage rooms for business records, wanted her own business. Starting your own business takes real belief in yourself and your idea. How did she take such a key step in her life?

1. After getting the idea, she thought about it for a few years until she felt sure that she wanted to go ahead with it.
2. She researched a similar company in Boston.
3. She began the new business in her home.
4. She did not give up when her new-business loan applications were turned down by local banks. One bank finally loaned her the money that she needed and introduced her to investors.

Her business offers a safe and useful service. It stores paper records for all kinds of companies, as well as computer tapes, microfilm, cassettes, and other materials. The records can be stored away from a firm's office site. As Jean Taylor describes her service: "It is one of those 'I wish I'd thought of that' businesses."

---

grams, systems, and fresh ideas for earning extra money. Ads and sales letters that promise to deliver this widely desired, "open sesame" pathway to the world of riches (or to at least a healthy degree of financial freedom) continually get good results.

After years of studying hundreds of these money plans and systems, I'm absolutely convinced that many who order them never try them out or even return the materials for refunds. They get hooked by the power of the ads and sales letters, but when they receive the product, they often decide they can't do what the plan calls for or they don't like certain aspects of the program. Perhaps more money than they have access to is required to put the plan into action. (In many cases, it is.) For any number of reasons, many buyers of these money-making plans do not follow through. But from the viewpoint of the mail-order operator who has sold them on the plan, the scheme has been a success, since so many orders have been received.

So always remember that human curiosity is a powerful thing. It motivates prospects to send you their orders. They want to know what the deal is, how the program works, whether it will honestly and truly help them to earn more money, whether it's right for them, legal, and if, in fact, they can do what the plan proposes.

When a prospect is thinking about sending in an order, these are the key questions he or she ponders:

1. Does it really work?
2. If I can follow the steps, can I make extra money this way?
3. Is it legal?
4. Can it be done where I live?
5. Can it be done on a part-time basis?
6. How much money will it take to start up?
7. Does it have the potential to bring me financial freedom?
8. Is it fresh and new or just another variation of hundreds of other plans, programs, and systems already being offered?
9. Will I be ripped off in some way?
10. Do I really want to know how the plan works badly enough to pay the asking price and send in an order?

If you can come up with a plan, system, or program that lures a prospect by responding effectively to such questions, you'll very likely have a smash winner on your hands, a real money-maker for your line, and one that will bring you a carload of orders. Shoot for a quality product as your number-one objective. Then try to determine how well your product answers the questions above.

"I'VE GOT THE NUMBERS THAT CAN CHANGE YOUR LIFE"

If you don't think the mailboxes of America are filled with all kinds of "number" pitches, then you haven't bought anything by mail in some time, or they've lost your name and address.

Every weekday brings at least three or four direct-mail letters to my mailbox, and many of them are trying to lure me into sending in my order for a "sure-fire" system of winning lottery numbers, a "new way" to win sweepstakes, a formula designed to bring more wins, or my astrological chart—if I will just send in my birthdate plus my order and fee.

Every gimmick in the world is used to get prospective mail-order buyers to open the envelope, read the letter and other materials, and send in an order.

I get so many of these "I can help you pick and use the right numbers" letters, with so many duplications of exactly the same offers, that these advertisers must be doing well. They wouldn't keep sending out their sales letters unless orders were flowing back to them.

Testimonial quotations from satisfied buyers are used in many of these sales letters. For example, one letter I got had this quote at the top of the page: "Thanks to you I won over forty thousand in the lottery. . . . I thank you so much." It was signed "Mrs. D."

Notice how only one initial was used. Initials are often used in testimonials, but prospects are on to this sometimes phony device. When only the initials appear, the truth of the quote is suspect. Don't think that testimonials are not helpful. They are. But it's far better to use the *full name* of the person providing the testimonial. If the person giving the testimonial is truly happy with a mail-order purchase, he or she isn't likely to object to his or her full name being used.

So if you plan to use testimonial quotes in your ads or sales letters, try to get the people who provide them to agree to let you use their full names. That will make the quotes much more believable.

Nearly all these "number" plans and systems offer some kind of free gift. This is often advertised via a 3 1/2-by-8 1/2-inch black-and-white card that may have a small drawing of a present or package, to represent the gift.

Among the pitches I've gotten recently was a "scientific system" for picking lottery numbers. The headline read, "458 People Have Been Able to Win at Least $300,000.00 Each Using the Same System." The large accompanying circular's headline read, "Win the Lottery—Right Now—Before It Shuts Down."

Funny thing: I ordered and tried this system several years back. I didn't have even one winning number, much less six of them. But it's interesting to know they're still in business. A lot of people must still be sending them orders.

You might do very well by offering some kind of plan or system to help buyers pick the right numbers. But such an offer needs to be fresh, different, and should provide some proof that it will really work.

Mail-order buyers are fed up with buying products that are pitched as "unique and entirely workable" only to discover, when they receive them, that they're like so many others—useless, unworkable duds.

You'll hear me saying this again and again in one way or another: Come up with products and services that are as good as the ads or sales letters that pitch them, and you can write your own ticket in mail-order. In fact, a key purpose of this book is to inspire and motivate you to do this very thing, to make your products and offers as good or better than the ads that sing their praises.

A LIFETIME OF HOMEWORK

Several years ago, a small display ad in a national magazine caught my eye. Intrigued by the ad, I sent my order in and was delighted to receive the product, a very handsome, two-color book, in just ten days. Already the product had won points with me. Most items you order take months to receive, so I was very pleased. Here was a mail-order company, a small one, that was filling its orders promptly and offering a very high-quality product.

I was very impressed by the book. The first half told how this particular mail-order operator, George W. Haylings, had gotten into the business after moving to California from his native Detroit. (Actually, George had experimented in mail-order publishing even as a kid in Michigan so he wasn't entirely new to the industry.)

Over the years, George built his company into a big success. He started with two- and three-page folios and progressed from there into booklets, books, and newsletters. George actually started what became his lifetime business in a tent, typing out material about odd, unusual kinds of businesses that were making people money. When his aunt in England sent him several pound-sterling notes, George used the money to run a small classified ad in *Mechanix Illustrated*. It was the middle of the worst depression this nation has ever known. To George's surprise, his first ad brought in a sizeable amount of orders and inquiries.

After that humble beginning, George went on to publish plans, manuals, and booklets until he went into the Army in 1942. George writes: ''It was there, as a sort of Sergeant Bilko in charge of the 'Orderly Room' that I wrote my first book, called *Discovered, 505 Odd Enterprises*.'' This book was very successful and led George to author 18 others between the late 1940s and 1960. ''By 1963 I had done so well that I more or less retired,'' he says.

The offer or product you sell by mail-order is vitally important. Your choice of offers must be narrowed down and carefully selected. In the next chapter, we'll take a look at this key decision you must make.

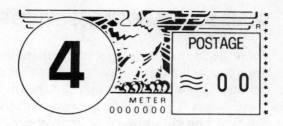

Choosing Your Offer Carefully

Unlike the lead character in the film *The Godfather*, who through his sons and associates made "offers that couldn't be refused," you face the challenge of coming up with offers that are right for mail-order, popular with buyers, and able to be sold at prices that will bring you a reasonable profit and that have the potential to bring repeat sales.

The point is that in the mail-order business, your offers can and may well be refused, unless they reach out and grab buyers and persuade them to send in orders.

A mail-order company without one or more strong, attractive offers is like Disney World minus Mickey Mouse. You really aren't in the mail-order business until you develop at least one sound, attractive offer that hits the target and makes potential customers reach for their checkbooks or credit cards.

So how do you know if and when you have a magnetic offer? The only way to really tell in this business is to test it, and then to test it again.

SOME SOUND BUSINESS STEPS FOR MAIL-ORDER

There are sound and practical business steps you can follow once you believe you have an offer that can bring in profitable results. These practical steps can mean the difference between success and failure, so I urge you to put them into action in the running and building of your mail-order company. These important steps include the following:

1. Stick to the basics.
2. Target your markets carefully.
3. Find out if others are selling the item successfully.
4. Get some outside opinions on your offer.

Stick to the Basics

What *are* the basics when it comes to mail-order offers? They are the tried and tested staple offers that have proved to be consistently popular and attractive to mail-order buyers. These staple offers include money-making plans of all kinds, health products such as vitamins, weight-reduction programs, how-to-do-it instruction guides ranging from ten or twenty up to hundreds of pages, self-teaching correspondence courses in a variety of subject areas, and all manner of products that increase the happiness quotient of buyers in some meaningful way, such as "art-of-living" guides on where to retire or how to live more happily and comfortably on less money.

For example, a strong seller in recent years has been the plastic "gut-buster" pull-up device that exercises your stomach. After the big success of books such as *How to Flatten Your Stomach*, I reasoned it was just a matter of time before companies would offer a variety of products designed to slim down the potbellies of America—and maybe the world.

Target Your Markets Carefully

Television was the main advertising medium used to sell the gut-busters, although I've seen ads for them in magazines and

SUCCESS STORY: Joe Sugarman

One of the kings of the mail-order business is Joe Sugarman, who sells high-priced microelectronic products. He uses full-size ads in leading publications and has become one of the richest operators in the mail-order industry.

Sugarman studied electrical engineering at the University of Miami. To help a local restaurant increase the number of its customers, he wrote an ad for the school paper, which proved to be so successful that Sugarman soon found himself helping other local businesses through his own small ad agency.

In the early 1970s, Sugarman raised about $12,000 and began to sell a small calculator in *The Wall Street Journal*. In only two weeks he counted a $20,000 profit. He used big display ads, and his calculator kept on selling. He then ran ads in many major magazines, and after three months he had realized a handsome net profit of $500,000. Sugarman hired some employees and opened an office and a warehouse in Northbrook, Illinois. Reportedly, his company now employs about 50 people and has become a top seller of home burglar alarms and digital watches.

---

newspapers as well. At about the time they began to be offered, I was beginning to fight the battle of the bulge, so I promptly sent in my $19.95 order. You know what? The gut-buster I received helped a lot to smooth down my stomach. Experts now say that these gut-busters will not completely eliminate midriff bulge, but they definitely do help and also greatly strengthen the abdominal muscles.

I still use the gut-buster I bought by mail-order, and I believe that using it five minutes a day does a lot to help keep a trim stomach, providing you also watch your diet and get enough other exercise. I certainly got my money's worth with that order. I'm sure that thousands or possibly tens of thousands of others have also been satisfied users of this right-on-the target product. It was a magnetic item. There was a large market of prospects for it, and the television commercials paid off with good results. At this writing, the gut-buster and products like it are still being sold on television mail-order commercials.

Are Others Selling the Item Successfully?

Most veteran mail-order operators already know that a good sign of a given product's likely success is the answer to one simple, but important, question: Is the product or service item currently being sold successfully by others?

In other words, does the item you have in mind for mail-order sales already have a history? Will you be selling a product that has proved it can bring in orders or will you be blazing a trail with some brand-new item never offered before?

Frankly, I believe one reason some mail-order operators fail to build their companies into successes is that they fall in love with one or more products and refuse to scuttle them when the bottom line shows that they're failures.

John Huston, the legendary film director, usually took on a new film assignment for one of two reasons: because of the money he was offered or because of his personal interest in directing it. In mail-order you don't have the same freedom of choice. One or two unwise product or service items can cost you a bundle if they don't sell. It costs you money to line up the product, produce or obtain a healthy supply of it, advertise, and fill your orders. So before a new item can even begin to start earning money, you've spent a lot to introduce it to your customers. It doesn't take a genius to realize that disastrous results with items you thought might fly can wipe you out of business.

This is where testing pays off. Test the new product ideas you get and watch the results carefully. Find out if other mail-order companies have sold the item, and whether they're currently doing so or if they've abandoned it. Answer some ads yourself for such items and study the sales letters or ads being used.

By doing the spadework before you launch a new item, you'll have a much better idea where you're going. Remember, shooting craps with new product ideas can be risky. There may be handsome profits to be made, but there may also be catastro-

WHAT TO SELL BY MAIL

Some of the best ideas for products can be picked up by browsing through the pages of publications such as *Income Opportunities*, *Popular Mechanics*, *Opportunity*, *The Star*, *New Business Opportunities*, *Wealth Secrets*, *The Wall Street Journal*, and others.

Some of the many products advertised, to name just a few, are a music scroll, an exerciser, a family-tree book and chart, a dog bed, rapid-reading recordings, a personalized rubber stamp, a coat-of-arms emblem, a secret money belt, reading glasses, an oxygen inhaler, and a vast assortment of how-to-do-it and money-making books, programs, and plans.

What do most of these successful mail-order products have in common? The first thing you notice is that they're a bit unusual. Most of the offerings have unique or otherwise attractive features. Many are items that you can't buy just anywhere. If the customer wants the product advertised, he or she may have no choice but to purchase it from a company selling it by mail—an enviable situation for the mail-order dealer.

---

phe lurking in the wings. Proceed with caution: Test, research, and study before jumping in on a whim or impulse. You may well be glad you did move cautiously.

Get Some Outside Opinions on Your Offer

Experts in the mail-order industry can sometimes be reached by mail, if you use the correct address. But even if you're unable to reach the people you want, you can definitely contact some of the leading magazines and newspapers in the field, such as *Income Opportunities* magazine, *The Wall Street Journal*, *Popular Science* magazine, *Opportunity*, and others. You can ask the advertising managers or departments of these publications if they believe you have a product that will pull in orders.

Authors of books on mail-order can also be written to, in care of their publishers. All mail is forwarded to them.

Another excellent idea is to ask some of your regular customers what they think of your new offer or product. Customers who have sent you orders previously are usually willing to respond with their opinions because they've dealt with your company and, you hope, have been pleased with the items they purchased. So they trust you and your company. You might choose a representative sampling from your current customer list and ask these buyers directly for their reactions to your new product or service.

When you solicit opinions on new offers, it's wise to send along a form the person can use to quickly check off his or her feelings about your new items. You should also enclose a stamped return envelope, since your customer is doing you a favor by responding.

Still another good bet is to seek the views of other mail-order operators. If you choose this route, however, just realize that you'll be exposing your new product ideas to companies that may be competing with you. Your competitors may like your idea so well that they may decide to sell it, or something similar, themselves.

YOUR BEST SHOT AT SUCCESS

My own experience, knowledge of the business, research, and the testimonials of other mail-order operators convince me that your best chance for real success will come by offering products that do the following:

1. Increase the customer's wealth.
2. Give the customer programs, systems, or plans for getting out of debt, planning better vacations, buying real estate, making more profitable and wiser investments, living a happier life, and other similar objectives. Remember, an enormous number of potential buyers out there are looking for smart new ways to add to their monthly and yearly incomes. Many of these are people who already have one key job, but who want to moonlight with a second (or even a third) way of generating money.

3. Improve the health or well-being of the customer.
4. Instruct the buyer how to make, create, learn, or do something of interest.
5. Make the buyer more fulfilled, contented, satisfied, and productive.
6. Promise a novelty item so curious, fascinating, or appealing that customers cannot resist buying.

Whenever you think about adding a new offer to your line, I urge you to turn back to this chapter and see if and how your new item measures up. Before rolling out a direct offer to prospects, test it and then test it again. Try to have a fairly good idea as to how possible buyers are likely to respond. Sometimes a test in a weekly newspaper can give an indication. Once you have this test information, you can either scuttle the idea or move ahead with it with some expectation that you have a winner. But your confidence will be greater if you test a number of times, not just once or twice, before coming out with a new offer.

PART II

Effective Advertising

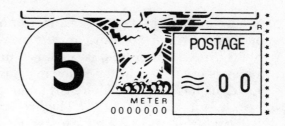

POSTAGE

≈ . 0 0

METER
0000000

Getting Your Product or Service Across

Whatever your existing line of products or services might be, your objective is to get it across to your prospects—to reach your market, make prospective customers want to buy your offer, and convince them to send in their orders.

In mail-order this is done through effective advertising. In many cases, other mail-order firms will be offering the same, or a similar, product or service, which means you have to come up with a strong, competitive strategy. Remember, a quality product is of the utmost importance.

THE RIGHT ATTITUDE TOWARD COMPETITION

How do your attitudes toward competition affect your opportunity for advancement? How much do your feelings about your competitors affect the success of your business? More than you might realize.

There are two basic reactions to competition. One is a response of anger, tension, and anxiety in which the competition (whoever or whatever it is) is seen as a threat. This attitude is sometimes expressed in the following ways: "It's her or me." "One of us has to go." "There isn't enough room in this town for both our companies." "They're highly competitive." "He'll cut his prices to the bone to get business."

In other words, one reaction to competition is negative. People who have this response are usually unhappy with the fact that competition exists. Often because of this attitude, such people end up doing poorly in the race for a job, new business, a prize, sale, award, promotion, money, new account, or whatever. They come out on the short end because of these negative feelings about competition. Their attitude may do much to short-circuit what might otherwise have been a winning performance or piece of work. Inner resentment and even bitterness toward competition may thus turn out to be destructive by preventing those who respond this way from doing their best.

The other, positive reaction to competition is certainly more healthy. In this response, competition is viewed with the attitude reflected in these statements: "May the best person win." "The company that can deliver the most will get the business." "I don't fear any competition because I know I've got the best product (or service) for the money." "The spirit of competition is alive and well." "My competitiveness brings out my best."

In other words, competition is seen as an incentive that keeps someone on his or her toes. If there were no competition—if everything in life were cut and dried—things would be awfully dull. Lack of competition would stagnate the growth and development that are vital to real success. No matter what is being sought (a prize, money, a sale, a job promotion, a company takeover, or whatever), a burning desire to attain that goal—which means a willingness to compete—is probably essential to superior performance.

Few people really go places or climb the success ladder by just thinking occasionally about what they want or by doing so only when the spirit moves them. It's when what you want becomes a burning desire, when you get no peace until you have it, that things really start to happen. As the old saying goes, "If you want something badly enough and think about it hard enough, you're very likely to get it'' (assuming, of course, that you also take active steps to attain it).

This means you have to welcome competition and view it as something that will keep you sharp and working and producing at your best—seeing it, in other words, as a catalyst to make you give it all you've got, turning in your maximum performance to get what you want, whatever it may be.

The real professionals in all fields welcome competition and even thrive on it. Competition adds flavor, challenge, excitement and gusto to any endeavor, including the fascinating mail-order business.

Calvin Coolidge, a U.S. president in the early years of this century, said, ''The business of America is business.'' The business of America is still business today, only more so. In this era of giant company mergers, takeovers, and high technology, the skill and ability to be a good manager are more vital than ever.

My own opinion concerning why companies stagnate, slip downward, lose business and customers, and in some cases go bankrupt can be expressed in two words: poor management. You've seen it, too. A great restaurant that has been prospering and packing them in begins to hit the skids. The reason is often a change in managers. A new manager comes in who may have a completely different view of daily operation than the previous manager did. Or the stock of a given company, once high, may drop like a wounded duck with a new manager at the helm. The same is true for baseball and football teams, governments, plants, schools and colleges, banks, motion picture studios, and so on.

So what does this mean for you? Simply that you must strive continually to be a first-class, front-line, up-to-date, and skillful manager. Let me say it this way:

- A quality mail-order manager stays constantly informed about changes, trends, and laws affecting the industry.
- A quality mail-order manager knows what effective advertising consists of, believes in it, and uses it regularly to achieve greater success.
- An aware mail-order manager remains a keen student of what makes people buy. The psychology, art, and science

of motivating prospects to send in orders are of great importance to this kind of manager.

- A quality mail-order manager constantly seeks out, re-searches, develops, and applies new and more dynamic ways to get a product or service across to the appropriate market.

This means keeping up with information regarding the strongest media to use for advertising, what kinds of ads or commercials get the job done best, the changing factors in consumers' lives, new techniques that bring good results, and more.

One fact cannot be stated too many times: You may have the most wonderful product or service item in the world, but if you don't let prospects know about it, what good is it? *Reader's Digest* grew by leaps and bounds because the magazine told the public about itself. The same is true of Sears, Westinghouse, Folger's Coffee, Delta Airlines, and many other companies you can name. These corporations got their products and services across to buyers, and the response that resulted meant con-tinual growth and new areas of success. In other words, you ignore getting your offers, products, and services across to possible buyers at your peril.

FINDING HIGH-QUALITY NAME LISTS

When purchasing name lists, you must be careful to distinguish between lists of *actual* buyers—those who have sent in orders—from those who have merely inquired for more details or infor-mation. Obviously, names of buyers—of people who spent $5.00, or $75.00, or more on mail-order items—are much more valuable.

The right mailing lists, containing the names of mail-order buyers of items similar to what you are offering, can produce a fortune. But I urge you not to jump in and buy too large a list at first. A wiser course of action is to mail sales letters to a sampling of 2,000 to 5,000 names drawn from a much larger list. You should have the results of your test within six weeks.

DIRECT MAIL CAN BE YOUR ROAD TO RICHES

1. You can have a fast-growing list of customers.
2. You can bring in more responses by direct mail than by any other medium.
3. You can make your sales package as simple or sophisticated as you wish. It can range from a one-page sales letter and reply card to a four-page (or longer), four-color letter, circular, and order form.
4. You can test your offers or products often. Different sales letters and combinations of sales literature can bring a variety of responses.
5. You can send out as many offers as you wish. And you can time your mailings to arrive at any time you want them to.
6. You can have more freedom in what you say in your direct-mail copy than you have in ads.
7. For extra sales, you can send new offers to your growing customer list time after time. That means you can build a thriving business from your own private list of customers.
8. You can focus on only those prospects who have responded to offers similar to yours. You can also send your mailings only to selected geographic regions.
9. You can address your offer to people using their names, making your sales technique much more personal. Unlike ads in print or on radio or TV, there is no "arena effect"—ads surrounded by other ads—when you use direct mail. Your prospects open their mail and there is your sales message, with no other competing ads to lure them away from what you have to say.

You need to be aware of some of the keys to using mailing lists effectively:

1. You have a choice of mailing lists to use.
2. You control the mailings. You can choose which day or week to send out your mailings and also the number of sales pieces that you send.
3. During the slow mail-order season (the summer months), you can discontinue mailings.

4. You can schedule short vacations for yourself around the times you don't send out any mailings. Some mail-order operators send out large mailings at selected times of the year and then take it easy, or focus their attention . elsewhere, the rest of the time.

5. You can mail three or four times a year to the growing customer list you'll be building from your business.

RESULTS FROM NAME LISTS

A cold list of names may pull a response of 1 to 4 percent. Your own customer list will be a much better result-getter for you. Treat that list with care and value.

When you mail to a cold list of names, you should send a four-page brochure (8 1/2 by 11 inches) plus a return envelope. Some mailers make the order form part of the sales letter; you can do this, or you can send a separate form.

An excellent way to keep up with sources of good mailing lists is to watch the issues of *Income Opportunities, Opportunity, The Wall Street Journal, Popular Science*, and other leading mail-order publications. *Direct Marketing* magazine includes the names of list-brokers you can contact for information on their lists.

For your use and reference, here are the names of some leading mailing-list brokers (I have not included addresses because these tend to change from time to time. You can obtain the current addresses by checking the *Yellow Pages* of the city involved):

Dunhill International Lists	New York, NY
Ed Burnett Consultants	New York, NY
Dependable Lists, Incorporated	New York, NY
William Stroh, Incorporated	New York, NY
Addressing Unlimited	Van Nuys, CA

If you know others in the mail-order business, they'll probably be happy to recommend a good list-source to you. You can also reply to some of the ads you see in mail-order publications and request information on the lists those companies offer.

WHATEVER YOU SELL BY MAIL

No matter what product or service you sell by mail, a good place for a test run or for a series of ads for an already-tested offer is the "Shop by Mail" section of *The Wall Street Journal*.

The readers and potential customers of "Shop by Mail" are consumers with good incomes, including some influential executives. If your product or service is attractive, is right for these prospects, and is effectively advertised, you should do well.

Some recent products for sale in the "Shop by Mail" section have included the following:

- Snacks
- Ties
- Tabacco products
- Silverware
- Crystal
- Nuts
- Knives
- Cars
- Shirts and shorts

Some list companies will refuse to allow you to test as few as 2,000 names. Many of them require a minimum purchase of 5,000 names. If that's the case, you may want to look further for companies that will agree to smaller rentals.

THE LOWEST-COST WAY TO START AND BUILD

The ideal way to get started with mail-order advertising is to use what I have come to refer to as the "star-studded jewels of mail-order." Experienced mail-order operators will know that I'm referring to classified ads. Many a mail-order operator owes his or her success to classified ads. Quite a few in the industry will admit that the classified part of their business not only formed the basis, the bedrock, on which their eventual success was built, but that they still use classifieds because these "little gems'' continue to earn their keep. Most of the successful people I have known in mail-order started with small classified ads and then expanded to small display ads, direct mail, and full-page ads.

Classifieds teach a lot about the business. They acquaint you with how to write headlines and ''teaser'' copy, and they teach you how to make every word pull its weight, how to say a lot in as few words as possible.

Classified ads can intrigue, motivate, and arouse the curiosity of prospects. And they can do it in a very few words. Running classified ads in a variety of mail-order publications helps you develop confidence, teaches which advertising categories are best for given products and offers, shows you which publications pull better, and much more—at a relatively low cost.

Classified ads cost more today than they used to, but they remain the least expensive way to start advertising and get a mail-order company launched. Most, if not all, of the super-stars of mail-order started with classifieds. I cannot recommend this route highly enough, if you're new to the business.

THE CHOICE TO DO LITTLE OR NO MAILING

A clear advantage of direct mail is the fact that you can have complete control over the size and frequency of your mailings. You can send out as few as a thousand or as many as 100,000, or more, pieces. Some very active direct-mailers send out a million pieces in one mailing. This obviously costs a great deal, so unless you're very sure you have a winner and you can afford the printing and postage costs, stick to smaller mailings. As I said earlier, a good-size mailing for testing a new offer is about 2,000 to 5,000 pieces. If the results are encouraging, you can roll out a mailing of 10,000, 50,000, or more. Some direct-mailers expect a return of 2 to 6 percent, but that assumes a very strong sales letter and package. Many who use direct mail on a regular basis are happy to pull a 2 or 3 percent response. Generally, the stronger your sales letter and direct-mail package, the higher your response will be.

Certain times of the year are better for mailings than others. The months of September and October are particularly effective times to get offers to prospects. Many consider January to be the single best month of the year for your offers to arrive in the mailboxes of prospective customers.

I urge you to skip the entire month of December, though. If you're fairly experienced in the business, you're no doubt already aware of this. Some mail-order people say they make sales in December, but as a rule it's a bad time to mail. Christmas is too near, and prospects are busy focusing on the approaching holiday. Many a direct-mail package is promptly thrown in the trash if it arrives during December. And the closer to Christmas a mailing is sent out, the more poorly it's likely to do. Stick to January-February and the September through November season as the best times for your mailings.

PRINT ADS

Strong, effective print ads are crucial to getting the message across about your product or service.

One fast way to improve the pulling quality of your print ads is to be alert for and to study magnetic headlines. By keeping an ongoing file of strong headlines, you will achieve two helpful and important results:

- You will develop a greater respect and appreciation for good headlines.
- You will gain more insight into the kinds of headlines that will work best for various types of ads.

Here are the ingredients that go into making a good print ad:

1. A gripping headline
2. An effective illustration (if it's a display ad)
3. Strong body copy
4. A coupon (many print ads include a coupon as part of the overall ad)

Ads are designed to do one thing: produce inquiries. I keep a thick file of what I call four-star headlines taken from a variety of print ads. A headline I've recently added to my file goes like this:

Headline: Death Before Poverty
Subhead: Immediately turn $20 into $2 million in 11 days exploiting over 2,000 financial institutions using my never before revealed statistical profile portfolio
Last punch line: I Took Their Cash, Take Your Share Now!

Now I have to be honest and say that my first impression on reading the ad above was that the subhead was far too long. I still think it's too long, but it's very strong. The curiosity of the reader is definitely aroused. Both the headline and subhead grab your attention. They certainly grabbed mine. Powerful headlines like this almost leap off the printed page and hit you right between the eyes. In other words, such a headline commands attention and leads you to read the entire ad.

THE PARAMOUNT PURPOSE OF A HEADLINE

Always remember, a headline's number-one purpose is to arouse attention and get a prospect to read the entire ad. The headline reproduced above succeeded in doing the job it was created for. It grabbed me, stirred my attention and interest, and made me want to read more.

If you can find the time each day, or at least once a week, to experiment with new headlines, your mail-order ads will be all the stronger for it. And that will translate into many more orders for your company.

By "experimenting," I mean that for a period of time you actually sit down and create new headlines, writing each one down and trying to come up with powerful phrases for both the main head and the subhead. If you can manage to do this for six months or a year, you'll notice a marked improvement in your print ads. They will be more gripping and will sparkle with power.

RADIO AND TELEVISION BOOST SALES

Radio and television ads are more accurately called commercials. While they are often expensive, they can quickly put an advertiser in the big leagues. Just as a full-page magazine ad can bring big profits to an advertiser (assuming the ad is a strong puller), a well-done radio or television commercial can bring a truckload of orders for your product offer.

Quite a few mail-order operators are content to limit their advertising to the leading mail-order magazines and newspapers. They do little radio and television advertising or none at all.

On the other hand, if one or more of your products or services seem well-suited for radio, television, or both, think about using a commercial.

One cable television program I saw showed a formerly bald man being interviewed by someone who was promoting a product called the Helsinki Formula. One after another, a group of men who used to be bald were asked for their opinions of the product. In every case, these apparently delighted men reported new hair growth after several weeks or months of using the Helsinki Formula.

Cliché or not, a picture is definitely still worth a thousand words. It was extremely effective, in this case, actually to show satisfied customers who had purchased, used, and were still using the product on a daily basis. The power of television lies in its ability to *show* and not just to tell.

I investigated and learned that this interview-style program received an avalanche of orders for the hair formula. Whether it really worked in every case or not, thousands of bald and balding men responded by sending in their orders. Now what guidelines does this suggest? What about these?

1. Assuming you can manage the cost, ask yourself if your offer is suitable for television or radio advertising.

2. Can the item be effectively shown on television? Or does it seem better suited to a sound-only commercial for radio?

3. Even 30-second television commercials can be expensive, but they are cheaper than full minute-long ones. You might settle for a 30-second spot, but you should realize it might be

difficult—and it certainly will be a challenge—to really say what you have to say and sell potential buyers on your offer in that brief an amount of time.

4. It will cost you much less to produce a radio commercial. You should take into account that the commercial could be used at key time slots to reach the market you're after.

If and when you decide your offer should be advertised on radio or television, an important point to remember is this: Some of the best results have come from interview-style program formats. If you can show a number of satisfied customers who have bought, like, and are currently using your product, you stand a good chance of really pulling in the orders. And once such a commercial or interview program is taped, you can run it as many times—and in as many time-slots—as you wish.

The decision to go on radio and television—and particularly television—really means going big time. Television sells an astronomical number of products and services. If you believe you're ready for it, and can handle the cost, you may well receive a staggering number of orders for your item. With the kind of returns television can bring, you might need only one or two winning offers to enjoy a bonanza of profits. Just be sure you have a winner—and one that's well-suited for TV—before going the television route.

Why People Buy by Mail

It's extremely important for a mail-order operator to understand why people buy by mail. I've already covered some of the reasons, but there are others worthy of discussion:

1. Convenience
2. "Not available elsewhere"
3. Privacy
4. Special price
5. Other inducements to buy
6. Magnetic headlines
7. Newness or freshness
8. Testimonials
9. Curiosity
10. The total effect of the ad

MAILING LIST BROKERS AND PRINT-AND-MAIL COMPANIES

These addresses were current at the time of writing. Bear in mind that they are subject to change.

List Brokers:

Addresses Unlimited
14621 Titus Street
Van Nuys, California 91402

The List Company
1200 Summer Street
Stamford, Connecticut 06905

Accredited Mailing Lists
3 Park Avenue
New York, New York 10016

Direct Media, Inc.
406 Chestnut Lane
Wayne, Pennsylvania 19087

Superior Mail Service
P.O. Box 290146
St. Louis, Missouri 63129-0146

Direct Media, Inc.
1216 N.W. Third
Oklahoma City, Oklahoma 73106

Alan Drey Company, Inc.
104 Crandon Boulevard
Miami, Florida 33149

Print-and-Mail Companies:

Northland Print and Mail
P.O. Box 45
Jericho, New York 11753

Long Island Print and Mail
P.O. Box 217
Merrick Long Island, New York 11566

Linda Enterprises
P.O. Box 690
Hallsville, Texas 75650

Target Mailing
132 West Crystal Avenue
Salt Lake City, Utah 84115

Metro Printing and Mailing, Inc.
12000 Sterling Boulevard
Sterling, Virginia 22170

Federated Mailing Systems
2720 S. Hardy
Tempe, Arizona 85282

Chiappone Mail Enterprises
936 11th Street, P.O. Box 1152
West Babylon, New York 11704-1152

Datatech Communications
351 Pike Boulevard
Suite 130, Dept. W-5
Lawrenceville, Georgia 30245

Ross International
P.O. Box 1683
Sacramento, California 95812

Triway Printers and Mailers, Inc.
301 North Frio
San Antonio, Texas 78207

THE FIRST REASON PEOPLE BOUGHT BY MAIL

You can probably easily guess the first reason people bought by mail during the early years of the industry. If you guessed convenience, you're right. And, today, convenience remains one of the top reasons thousands of buyers send in their orders by mail.

Think about it. It's a lot easier to fill in a coupon or order form, write out a check, place them in an envelope, and drop it in the mail than it is to go out shopping. No doubt about it. At one time the Pony Express was the quickest way to get a letter to the West Coast. Today, letters are flown there on big jets.

The early mail-order buyers quickly realized how much easier it was to order items by mail. Postage in those early years was a few pennies per letter. But even when first-class stamps reach 30 or 50 cents (and I expect they will go that high one day), mail-order will still be a convenient way to buy.

"Shop by mail in the comfort of your home" is the phrase in vogue today, and mail-order companies sell an unbelievable variety of products, plans, services, courses, and other items. There's something for every potential buyer in the world of mail-order.

"NOT AVAILABLE ELSEWHERE"

Prospective customers are motivated to buy without delay if, when they read your ad or sales letter, they discover that the item offered cannot be obtained anywhere else. This says to the prospective buyer that the product or service item is an *exclusive* one. "Not available elsewhere" communicates to possible buyers that the product cannot be purchased in the stores. In fact, it can only be bought through the mail-order company that ran the ad or sent the sales letter.

If your offer is unique and, as far as you know, truly not for sale anywhere else, you have every right to use this magic phrase in your ad and sales-letter copy. You would be foolish not to use it.

"Not available elsewhere" acts as a booster. It helps to convince prospects that your offer is special . . . and that if they want it they had better take action immediately. This useful phrase also carries the implication that the supply of the item might run out at any time. So if the rest of your ad or sales letter has created a desire for the item, the prospect gets the idea he or she had better send in an order promptly so as not to be left out.

You can test the power of this phrase yourself with one of your present offers. If it truly is not for sale elsewhere, then make sure you state this clearly in your ad or direct-mail letter. See if the number of sales doesn't increase when you use this phrase.

A major reason thousands of customers purchase an item through the mail is because they are convinced they can't get it in retail stores. It's as simple as that. "Not available elsewhere" prompts the customer when it comes to making a buying decision. Anything that helps you motivate buyers to act now is valuable. So be sure to make strong use of this psychological tool. It's a real prodder. It cuts through procrastination and can dramatically increase your mail-orders, sales, and profits.

WHY YOUR PRODUCT OR SERVICE IS DIFFERENT

The differences between your products and the offers made by others may be strong reasons why people will buy from you. Ask yourself the following questions:

1. How is my product different?
2. Does it have a better price? A better value? Is it more durable, or does it work more effectively than competing products?
3. What elements make it unusual (the way it's made, the style, colors, size, odd features, practical usefulness, informational value, etc.)?

In your ads you should strive to accent the different quality of what you are selling. Say just enough to whet their curiosity, but still communicate that your offer is somehow better than others, somehow different. This is obviously more important to do if you're selling something that other mail-order firms also offer.

In your sales letter or brochure, focus on telling the prospect what your product or offer *is not* and not on what it actually is. This leaves them guessing.

How do you communicate the idea that your item is different without using a lot of words? The following words and phrases should be useful to you:

- Out of the ordinary
- Offbeat
- Nothing else like it
- First time revealed
- Unusual
- Uncommon
- Unique

MAGNETIC, ATTENTION-GRABBING HEADLINES

I keep emphasizing headlines because they are so absolutely vital to your success. A powerful headline caught my eye just a little while ago, and I will probably send in an order to see what this material is all about. Again, you should make it a definite habit to save and file any appealing headlines. If a headline makes you want to send in an order, you can probably be sure it's having the same effect on many others. Here is the headline that grabbed my attention:

> *Headline:* Newly Discovered Secret: U.S. Employment Markets Will Make You a Millionaire
> *Subhead:* Recently, I Discovered a Very Unique Process for Which Anyone Can Easily Make Hundreds of Thousands or Even Millions of Dollars Starting Immediately

The above headline appeared in one of the magazines for opportunity seekers. It's pie-in-the-sky and sounds too good to be true, but so do most of the other large ads in these magazines. Remember that your goal is to offer a quality product or service. Your ad will draw in customers, but it won't retain them.

THE SIX MOST DEADLY CAUSES OF DIRECT-MAIL DISASTER

Consultant Robert Bly has had a lot of experience in the mail-order industry. Here is his list of pitfalls to avoid when advertising by direct-mail:

Why do so many powerfully written and brilliantly conceived direct-mail packages bomb so frequently? The reason is that too much emphasis is placed by clients on creative and not enough on other key factors which are far more influential in determining a mailing's success.

What are these factors? Here, in my experience, are the six most common reasons why direct-mail packages fail:

1. *The product.* Unlike consumers, who frequently buy on impulse, business-to-business prospects buy only those products or services that meet their needs, help them succeed, or solve a specific problem.

Many marketers will insist on going ahead with a mailing even when it is obvious that no one will want their product.

Frequently clients come to me with one or more of the following:

• A product that is not what the customer wants and will not meet his or her needs
• A product that meets their needs—but not more efficiently or cost-effectively than other, better products now available
• A product designed to provide a benefit the customer doesn't care about or solve a problem the customer does not feel is important
• A product that solves a problem—but the customer is not aware he has the problem, and educating him about the problem is too difficult to accomplish through the mail
• A product or service that is too complex or conceptually different to be explained in copy

In all of these cases, direct-mail will probably not be successful, no matter how well-written the copy.

2. *Market.* The second most common cause of direct-mail failure is not identifying the target market so proper mailing lists can be selected and tested.

Here are some common situations:

• The client has a product that provides an obvious benefit, but he does not know which industries have the most pressing need to acquire that benefit.

• The client wants to target certain types of companies, but does not know which job titles or functions would be responsible for evaluating his product or service.

• The client knows which industries and job titles he wants to reach, but cannot articulate how the sales presentation should be tailored to present the most appropriate benefits to each particular audience.

To succeed in direct mail, you must have a clear picture of what you are selling, who you are selling it to, and the reasons why they should buy it.

You must be able to tell your agency or copywriter which markets you want to reach, who within a company should receive the mailing, and the manner in which the presentation should be slanted toward each segment of the market.

3. *Lists.* Just because you have properly identified a target market doesn't necessarily mean there's a list of such people available. And if you don't have a list, you can't do direct response advertising.

Sometimes there is a list, but it is not large enough to justify the time and expense of doing a mailing.

In specialty markets, there may be only one list available, and if that list bombs, you have no place else to go.

With more and more business-to-business marketers experimenting with one-step (mail-order) vs. two-step (lead generating) mailings, the lack of good response lists in the business area has become a major problem. In my experience, compiled lists seldom produce good results for mail-order offers.

If list suppliers do not conduct sufficient research or provide enough background information on lists for decision-making purposes, most business-to-business list users are not knowledgeable enough to realize the mistake being made.

4. *Price.* Many business-to-business marketers do not realize that the business buyer, like the consumer, is tremendously price-conscious. Although it is true the business prospect is not paying out of his own pocket, he still cares very much how his company's money is spent.

If you do not believe that price is important, take any subscription package and mail it with the decimal moved one place to the right.

Compare the pull of $28.9ε for 12 issues vs. $289.50 and see if price makes a difference.

For new products, I usually recommend testing three prices: low, medium, high. For a $499 software package, we might test $399, $499, $599. If $599 is the winner, we test $599 vs. $699.

5. *Offer.* The structuring of the offer demands careful attention and planning, yet for many business-to-business marketers, it is merely an afterthought.

In lead-generating, you will get the best results by allowing the prospect to select either a hard offer or a soft offer. The hard offer is an initial meeting, estimate, consultation, or some similar event involving personal contact—either face-to-face or via telephone. The soft offer is an offer of a free booklet, report, or other printed information.

How can you make a mail-order offer stronger and, thus, increase response?

* Add "bill-me" as a payment option
* Accept credit card orders via a toll-free 800 number
* Structure the price as a time-limited discount (e.g., if you want the customer to send you $399, set the regular price at $499 and give a $100 discount in your mailing)
* Add a premium as an incentive for prompt payment (example: if selling an eight-cassette tape album, advertise it as a six-cassette program with two extra free bonus tapes given as a premium for prompt payment)
* Allow the customer to keep the preimum even if he returns the product.

6. *Testing.* Keeping track of results and testing various strategies and approaches is the only way to determine what works best, yet few business marketers are enthusiastic about testing.

In my opinion, the four most important things to test are:

* Lists
* Offer (including price and discount structure)
* Package format (e.g., self-mailer vs. letter package, personalized vs. non-personalized, letter and brochure vs. letter only, #10 package vs. 6-by-9-inches vs. jumbo format, teaser approach vs. blind envelope, etc.)
* Sales appeals (key benefits used in teasers, headlines, and opening paragraphs of letters)

Here are some other attention-grabbing headlines that have caught my eye recently:

- I know you are ready to have all the good things you want . . . I can help you.
- How can we expect our people to connect if our computers can't?
- Before you find yourself talking to your copier, talk to Kodak!
- There's a time for believing in yourself . . . That time is now!!!
- Start playing the world's richest lottery free!

"FIRST TIME REVEALED" PROGRAM

Another helpful phrase can increase the number of orders you receive, and therefore your profits. You sometimes see this short phrase at the very top of a full-page ad or a sales letter. Even classified advertisers use it in their copy. This phrase is "first time revealed."

If, in fact, your product or service has never, as far as you know, been revealed to the public before, you should definitely use the words to convince even more buyers to send you their orders. Here are some variations you might also use, depending on which best applies to your offers:

- First Time Revealed Program
- No Comparison With Any Other Plan
- Nothing Else Like It
- Limited Number Available
- My Program Has Never Before Been Released
- You'll Get in on the Ground Floor
- Never Offered Before
- This Is an Entirely New Method
- Exclusive System
- Newly Discovered

You should experiment with some of these phrases to see which ones bring the best results. The psychological power of such phrases is stronger than you might realize. Potential buyers like to know they're among the first ones to learn of your offer. Believing they are ahead of the pack, or "getting in on the ground floor," is appealing to them. It adds just that much more weight to the case for sending in an order. Buyers in general are attracted by the idea that something is exclusive, and their discovery of your offer before it has "gone down the pike" stimulates them to buy.

So when you honestly have something brand-new or never before revealed, communicate that fact by using that phrase or one similar to it. It increases customers' desire to see the item for themselves.

TESTIMONIALS HELP CONVINCE BUYERS

If a neighbor or relative dropped by your house and told you about a purchase he or she made and how pleased he or she was with it, do you think that might influence you to buy it too? If so, then you have a good idea of the power of testimonials in making sales.

Testimonials are the big guns in the arsenal you're compiling to get prospects to send in their orders to your company. Here are two examples of different types of testimonials taken from leading mail-order publications:

> *A direct-quote testimonial:* Astounding . . . Pure genius! To be quite honest I didn't expect much due to the low price. But I must say that I have never received better value! You actually understated the power of your plan! Truly unique.

In a direct-quote testimonial, the person's first name and last initial appear, along with his or her home city and state. Sometimes only the state is given.

> *Indirect testimonial:* One man in his thirties from California is making $90,000 a week with this method.

Notice that in the indirect testimonial, the good results achieved by one or more customers are paraphrased or reported indirectly. (Note also that the testimonial reproduced above sounds too good to be true, or too pie-in-the-sky to believe!) A direct-quote testimonial obviously has more believability, power, and influence on a prospective buyer than a secondhand report of how someone is doing with the item, which may or may not be true.

So where can you get good, believable testimonials? Well, right from your growing list of customers who are happy (you hope) that they bought from you.

When you send out new offers to your existing customer list, you can send along a form asking for their endorsement of your product. The best candidates for testimonials are those who have bought several items from you and are on your ''A'' master list of number-one customers. Some of them will probably be happy to fill out the form you send asking for their written statements of satisfaction. Be sure to send a *simple* form that your customers can fill in quickly, sign, and return to you promptly. Then you can legally and accurately quote what they said about your product.

The form need only contain spaces for the following:

Date
Name
Address
City-State-Zip
Specific Product Item Purchased
Customer's Endorsement/Statement about Product (Please write clearly or print your comments on, reaction to, and opinion of the product.)
Signature (at bottom of form)

Some very effective ads only use one or two strong testimonials. Other ads use none at all. The question in many a prospect's mind is whether the testimonial used is an honest and legitimate one and not a fictional recommendation created by the advertiser.

You should try to use only reliable, believable quotes from satisfied customers who have bought and liked your products. Don't make up testimonials because it's always possible that a prospect may ask for proof of a quoted endorsement. Such a prospect might ask to see your original copy of the endorsement. This isn't likely, but it has happened. If you have the dated and signed original forms from those customers who agreed to endorse your product items, you're safe.

In short, definitely use powerful testimonials whenever you can. They make strong evidence to back up your claims. Just be certain they are accurate and true statements from people who were happy they bought from your company.

Used correctly, wisely, and accurately, testimonials have real power to increase the number of orders you receive. Think of them this way: Testimonials are TNT power to make your company's sales and profits explode.

THE CURIOSITY APPEAL SHOULD BE STRONG

Don't you forget it: The human animal is curious by nature. As an advertiser, you should make it your business to become an expert in the art, and some would say the science, of appealing to curiosity.

Look over the last dozen or so ads you've run (classified, space, half-page, full-page) or your recent direct-mail sales letters and test them for basic curiosity appeal. Is it there? Or is an appeal to the prospect's curiosity missing from the copy?

Have you ever thought about what led you into the mail-order business? One of the influencing factors was probably curiosity. Something made you curious about mail-order, how it works, the business of running ads for products and services, and your chances of achieving success with your own mail-order company. What made you curious may have been ads you had answered, the products themselves, a book on mail-order, or perhaps an article about mail-order companies and the lucrative business mail-order can be. Or you may have heard someone speak about the business, its bright future, and the prosperity many entrepreneur-types are building inside the

THE STRONGEST HUMAN INCENTIVE

Ad genius Claude Hopkins, author of *Scientific Advertising*, said that "curiosity is one of the strongest human incentives." People today want bargains as never before, especially in the midst of changing prices, on-and-off-again inflation, and economy jitters.

Mind you, consumers do not want things to be "cheap." There's a definite difference between something being a bargain and something being cheap. As Hopkins puts it so well, "People want to feel that they can afford to eat and have and wear the best."

Human psychology is complex. Try to learn how to arouse a prospect's curiosity, for there is real selling power in this valuable ability. Strive to discover why consumers act as they do. Learn about the underlying processes—the drives, emotions, and attitudes—that cause people to respond as they do.

Realize, too, that prospects don't always think or act as they say they do. Often they themselves are not fully aware of the real reasons for their actions.

Strive not only to keep up with information about your product; also try to keep up with life itself. By this I mean that you should take note of what makes consumers stop and look, what attracts them, appeals to them, and what makes them buy. That kind of knowledge is power in the business world.

Hopkins certainly knew a great deal about the fine art of writing advertising copy. More importantly, he knew that advertising is first and foremost a business.

---

industry. In time, your curiosity motivated you to consider starting a mail-order firm of your own.

So in a very real sense, your own personal curiosity was a major motivating influence on your decision to try your luck in mail-order.

If you can see the role curiosity played in drawing you into the business, you can certainly understand the vital importance of making sure your ad and sales-letter copy appeals to people's curiosity. What is it that makes people want to know more? What is it that intrigues ad and sales-letter readers and gets them to make that all-important decision to buy? Here are some of the answers:

1. The curiosity to know what the product or offer is
2. The curiosity to know if one could make money with the item (if it's a money-making system, plan, or program)
3. The curiosity to know what the item looks like, how it works, and if it does what it's supposed to do
4. The curiosity to discover what the information is regarding the product

If you can word your ad and sales-letter copy to appeal to such curiosity, you will definitely receive orders, probably a lot of them. Be on the lookout for these appeals whenever you read other companies' ads and sales letters, and learn from them.

YOUR AD IS THE MOST IMPORTANT ELEMENT

That the strength of your ads is the essential ingredient in your recipe for creating sales is one of the most important statements in this book. I cannot stress it too much. If potential buyers are not led by your ad to take action and send in their orders, then it makes no difference at all if you have an entire line of wonderful products.

Your number-one objective is to convince the readers of your ad or sales letters to send in their orders to your company. What this clearly means is that to become an established, successful mail-order company, you absolutely must develop and master the art of producing powerful ads and sales letters.

Even classified ads in some of the leading mail-order publications like *Popular Science* and *Popular Mechanics* cost nearly $10.00 a word these days. So a 20-word ad can easily run to $200.

If and when you go to half-page and full-page space ads, you'll be paying thousands and thousands of dollars just to run your ad in one issue. With this much money at stake just for the ad, you'd better be sure you've got a winner that will pull in lots of orders.

THE CATALOG SHOPPER

*T*he *Wall Street Journal* has a section that's just right for advertising your catalog. It's called "The Catalog Shopper." Some items advertised recently in "The Catalog Shopper" include the following:

- A catalog of 100 styles of curtains
- An innovative gift catalog
- A free, 240-page catalog of cameras, electronic goods, audio and video equipment, fax machines, computers, jewelry, watches, and more
- A free color catalog of shirts
- *The Very Finest in Golf*, a free competitive-golf catalog
- A free catalog with special sales prices on playsets manufactured in Maine
- *Best-Sellers on Cassettes* (free brochure offered)
- A free color catalog of outdoor clothing
- A free catalog of fine, imported hand-rolled cigars
- A free brochure of polo shirts
- A catalog listing over 350 chrome-plated bronze hood ornaments ($3.00)
- Information on diamond substitutes (small charge)
- A maternity clothes catalog ($3.00 for catalog, refundable with order)
- A free catalog of hand-engraved family crest rings
- A free catalog of recorded books (450 titles)

The thing to do is test your ads before making commitments to run half- or full-page ads in major magazines. Test in the following ways:

1. Test in Sunday newspapers. You have a lot of newspapers around the country to select from.
2. Test in magazine classified sections, where the rate per word isn't too high.
3. Test the ad with 2,000, 5,000, or more names from a list-source.
4. Test in daily newspapers. (Dailies, however, are usually poor barometers of an ad's quality. If you wish to test in

newspapers, you might want to stick with the first suggestion of trying the mail-order sections of Sunday newspapers.)

I personally believe that you should offer products or services that are at least close to being as good as the ads you run for them.

While it's true that your ad is the most important element in your success, this doesn't mean you can slip by with a shoddy product. If you do, the people who buy from you will feel angry and ripped off.

Believe me, there are already enough mail-order operators out there with stunning, gripping ads and terrible products. They may take in some money for a period of time, but consumers don't appreciate being cheated. They may order once from such outfits, but it's doubtful they'll ever order again.

The way to gain high profits, satisfied customers, and lasting achievement in this business is to stand behind your advertising with the very best products and services you can produce. In other words, always strive to make your offers as good as, or almost as good as, the ads you run to sell them.

After all, you do receive the customer's money before he or she can see your item. So there's definitely trust implied. If people who buy by mail get burned too many times, they may be lost to the industry forever. The shoddy, careless operator doesn't mind this, figuring that any lost customers are easily replaced by new buyers. Word of mouth does travel, however, and these careless operators may be killing their own business, if only slowly.

There are ethics you should follow in this business if you want to build a solid reputation and still be around ten or 20 years from now. Somehow, most of the shoddy mail-order operators fall by the wayside sooner or later. The law of cause and effect, it seems, pertains to the business world as much as to life in general.

I urge you to reach for high standards as you run your business: You will only grow more successful and prosperous in the long run. Have the integrity to offer quality products and services that you wouldn't mind any person in your family buying. The Golden Rule most definitely applies to the mail-order business.

PART III

Finding Your Proper Growth Rate

Be Consistent With Your Product

Once you've developed a product or service you believe in, you must make up your mind to stick with it until either you obtain success or you're forced to abandon it and try something else.

The secret of the success of the "short paragraphs for money" course discussed in Chapter 1 was the strong *consistency* behind the product. The man who developed this product didn't just try a few ads for several months and then stop. He advertised his product consistently, month after month, in the mail-order sections of many different magazines and newspapers. Almost without exception, his classified ads for the course were the same time after time.

The most successful ads are those that run again and again, month after month, and often in many different publications. In fact, to discover which ads are doing well, take note of those that appear time and again in issue after issue of leading magazines and newspapers. Advertisers don't keep running the same ads unless they're working and producing inquiries and orders. Advertising is too expensive to keep running ads that don't pay off.

TODAY'S FOCUS ON INCREASED SPECIALIZATION

These days, there is a focus on greater specialization every-where, and this trend is reflected in hundreds of specialized publications. Here are just a few of them:

- *Tow-Age*
- *Vehicle Leasing Today*
- *High-Tech Selling*
- *Glass Digest*
- *The Mini-Storage Messenger*
- *Video Business*
- *Candy Industry*
- *National Petroleum News*
- *Soybean Digest*
- *Beauty Age*

In other words, many new publications have cropped up to appeal to the special interests of specific consumers.

There are many different types of advertising copywriting, including ad agency, direct-mail, retail, and mail-order copywriting. If you're running a mail-order company, you will most likely specialize in mail-order copywriting. It's possible that later, after you have gained experience in direct mail, you may expand your copy work. But for the moment you'll mainly be concerned with classified, display, and direct-mail copy. Many mail-order operators confine their copywriting work to classified and space ads, but some eventually branch out to do direct mail, radio, and even cable television copy.

THE DANGERS OF EXPANDING TOO QUICKLY

Newcomers to mail-order and those with only a little experi-ence should beware of trying to expand their businesses too quickly. It's natural to want to build a successful company fast,

GUIDELINES FOR A SUCCESSFUL COMPANY: DREAM BIG

D ream no small dreams. Zero in on the big ones. The greater your dream, the better you will have to do and the farther you will have to reach to achieve it. Do something to realize your dream of mail-order success each and every day, even if all you can manage is just to think about it. That in itself is something. Sooner or later your mind will suggest specific courses of action you can take to move closer to making your dream come true. The world belongs to dreamers.

---

but it usually takes time to achieve this goal. Here are some pitfalls to try to avoid:

1. Don't overstock on an item, unless you're sure you've got a winner and fully expect orders to flow in constantly. Caution: This is one pitfall that drives many out of the business every year. They get overconfident about their products (often their very first offers), overstock them—perhaps going out on a financial limb to do so—and then find themselves stuck with a glut of product and not enough orders to move it. Don't let yourself fall into this trap. Test your offer a number of times first. Make sure it will pull in enough orders to justify the stock you have on hand and bring you a profit after your costs and expenses are paid.

2. By trying to grow too quickly, you will have to rush your ads and place too many of them, which may result in most of them doing poorly. It's far better to go slowly, planning each step carefully in advance and only then moving ahead. Some people come into the business thinking it's a get-rich-quick opportunity and go wild trying to do everything overnight.

3. Some who come into mail-order try to launch several offers at the same time. It's more practical to expand slowly, adding one item at a time. Focus your attention on one product or service and do all you can to get it established before trying to add others to your line. In other words, to reverse an old cliché, put all your eggs in one basket (one product item) and

then watch that basket until the item is established and constantly bringing in orders before going ahead with a new item.

REWARD YOUR EMPLOYEES AS YOU GROW

A great many mail-order operations are one- or two-person companies. But as your company grows more successful, you may want to hire some more part-time or full-time employees. If you reach the point where you have so many orders and inquiries coming in that you just can't get them all filled and responded to promptly, then it's time to think about hiring other workers to help you.

One successful California mail-order company uses teenagers to help stuff and seal envelopes. Many students are grateful for the chance to work on weekends or for a few afternoons or weeknights.

Many companies are content to remain fairly small. Others aim for a medium level of growth. And still others seek to grow as large and busy as possible. If you set your sights on this last option, and your company becomes increasingly successful, getting busier and busier with more and more orders and inquiries being received, you should reward your employees with better salaries and fringe benefits.

So keep all this in mind. As your company gets larger, you will have to deal with the following issues:

- More orders to fill
- More inquiries to answer
- More ads to place
- More records to maintain and paperwork to do
- More supplies to buy
- Higher postage costs
- Higher printing expenses
- More stock to carry
- More part-time or full-time employees to pay

CHECK OUT NEW BUSINESS IDEAS AND PLANS

During your company's growth process, you should make it a point to find the time to look over new business plans and

MAXIMS FOR EXECUTIVES

DIRECTNESS

"Directness. That's what works for me. I am very direct. Maybe to some people that's a defect, but that's the way I am. I generally don't sugarcoat the way I feel, and I am constantly in situations where I am very blunt and direct."

—Peter G. Scotese, Chairman, Executive Committee
Springs Industries, Inc.

IMPATIENCE

"One of my key characteristics is impatience. Sometimes that is a plus, but more often it is something that I have had to cope with. I am very conscious of this—for one thing, my wife reminds me of it with great regularity. Recognizing fully that I have this tendency, I have had to develop techniques to keep me out of trouble, ways to make my style yield results."

—James R. Martin, Chairman
Massachusetts Mutual Life Insurance Company

CHOOSING THE RIGHT PEOPLE

"In these difficult business times—and with our rapidly changing technology—you have to rely more on people and less on organization. Choosing the right people is essential. If you don't have smart, professional people, you can have the best organization in the world, but it will not work."

—Marisa Bellisario, Managing Director and Chief Executive Officer
Italtel Societa
Italiana Telecomunicazioni

---

ideas. Be consistent with your present offers, but explore other possibilities at the same time. What I'm advocating here is simply *research*. While sticking with whatever you're already selling, you can also be thinking about, and researching, other ideas and plans for the future. In this way, you will always have a new candidate (product or service offer) waiting in the wings.

Being consistent also means being ready to inject new life into a product that has grown stale or tired. Here are some specific ways to get new life into old products that seem to be going nowhere:

1. Find special-purpose markets where the product is unknown. Example: A nut-and-bolt company placed its products in auto-supply stores to be used as fasteners for license plates.

2. Think up some new twist or angle for using your product. This may be done by changing the package, or maybe by varying the size of the item. Uncover or develop some new convenience that the product offers. Does it last longer or work better under pressure than another product? Is it more durable? There are other conveniences there if you look for them.

3. Ask your customers if they have found any other uses for the product.

4. Try introducing the product to a different audience. Example: TWA transformed a poor season into a profitable one when it began to promote the idea of international travel to people who had never been to Europe. This idea greatly increased its profits.

5. Examine the product from every possible angle and strive to originate new uses for it. Are you overlooking any benefits it offers?

OFFERS WITH REPEAT SALES HELP YOU PROSPER

Many mail-order companies make their real profits in repeat sales. They may only break even on the first sale, but the follow-up sales to the same customers build profits.

Current issues of leading mail-order publications run ads for the following products or services that lend themselves to repeat-sales possibilities:

- Eyeglasses
- Rubber stamps
- Printing services
- Baseball cards

- Lists of mail-order buyers (for rent)
- Catalogs
- Newsletters
- Books
- Skin creams
- Credit cards
- Recipes
- Wine
- Jewelry
- Lingerie
- Job directories
- Bumper stickers

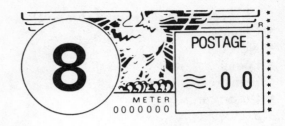

Keeping Track of the Competition

One absolute must in your mail-order business is the constant need to keep up with what your competition is doing. You don't run your business in a vacuum. You can benefit in important ways by knowing what other mail-order companies are offering, how similar their items are to yours, and the quality and effectiveness of their products.

A PROGRAM FOR KEEPING UP WITH THE COMPETITION

How can you best keep track of competing companies and their offers? Here are the elements of a useful program for keeping up with the competition:

1. Read your competitors' ads.
2. Analyze the copywriting appeal of their ads.
3. Find out if they offer a guarantee.

4. Do your competitors try to sell items directly from their ads, do they use the inquiry-and-follow-up method, or both?
5. What kind of advertising does your competition use? Only classified or both classified and display ads?
6. Are their products or services attractive, quality offers?
7. Do their ads use color?
8. Do your competitors' products lend themselves to repeat sales?
9. Do your competitors' sales letters include an order form as part of the letter or is the form separate?

Read Your Competitors' Ads

A number of times in this book, you have been advised to read your competitors' ads. If you're a mail-order operator, or expect to be, there's no getting around the need to read the ads placed by other mail-order firms. You can learn a lot from a regular reading of other mail-order ads. Be sure to do it.

Analyze the Copywriting Appeal of Their Ads

Don't be content with just quickly scanning the ads run by other mail-order firms. Go over the ads' copy and figure out what kinds of appeals are being used. There are lower-price appeals, appeals to the desire for having one's own business, to make more money, to get more fulfillment from life, to travel, to receive recognition, to be informed or entertained, to be more creative, well-liked, and a host of other universal desires. Ask yourself how your competition communicates these appeals in their ads.

Find Out If They Offer a Guarantee

If your competition is offering a guarantee, what kind is it? Are their guarantees good for two weeks, a month, six months, a year, or longer? Find out, too, if it's difficult to get a refund from

SELF-SCORING TEST ON AMBITION

Ambition is the fuel power behind many career successes. Ambition is a person's desire to reach out for more, to get ahead, to realize one's dreams, to "go for it." Champions in life, whatever the field, have an abundance of the magic elixir called ambition, but everyone can develop more ambition. The following test will let you see what present level your ambition is at.

Answer the following questions as best you can with either a Yes or a No. To score your performance, refer to the directions that follow the test.

1. Do you sometimes feel that you are not making enough progress in your job or in life in general?

2. Are you willing to work several hours each night and on weekends in order to get ahead?

3. When you achieve one of your goals, do you start moving toward the next one on your list?

4. Do you make a conscious effort to learn from your failures and mistakes?

5. If the opportunity came along to latch onto a rising star (possibly some person on the way up), would you do so?

6. Do you often read about or study subjects of interest to you?

7. Do you agree that a person can become more ambitious by making an act of will and then backing up that decision with action?

8. Would you be willing to change careers (possibly giving up job security) in order to get into work more to your liking?

9. Are you presently using all or most of your abilities and talents to forge ahead?

10. Do you think that people in general are more likely to succeed if they enjoy the work they do?

11. Have any past failures in your life made you more determined to achieve success?

12. Do you find the idea or goal of shooting for the top both exciting and challenging?

13. If it meant career advancement, would you be willing to move to another city or country?

14. Does the idea of working for yourself (in some form of self-employment) interest you?

15. Do you look for new ways in which you can be of more help to your present boss or superior?
16. Do you maintain a list of things you intend to accomplish in the future?
17. Do you often create, consider, and experiment with new plans designed to help you reach your objectives?
18. Have you set one or more deadlines for attaining your major goals?
19. Do you genuinely value the use of time and feel guilty on those occasions when you waste it (or believe that you've wasted it)?
20. Do you use slogans and positive statements written out and carried on index cards in order to keep yourself motivated with thoughts of victory and success?

DIRECTIONS FOR SCORING YOUR TEST ARE ON THE NEXT PAGE.

---

them on product items that are returned. Note: Some mail-order companies state guarantees in their ads or sales literature, but actually trying to get a refund from them can sometimes be like pulling teeth.

Do Your Competitors Try to Sell Items Directly From Their Ads?

Do they sell straight from ads, or do they use the inquiry-and-follow-up method, or both? The inquiry-and-follow-up method involves running ads that offer free literature on the product or that ask for a small amount of money (often $1.00) for sending full details to the inquirer.

What Kind of Advertising Does Your Competition Use?

Do they use only classified or both classified and display ads? Do they use direct mail at all? By keeping your eyes open and watching what competing companies are doing, you will learn which firms confine their advertising to classifieds and which ones use a double, or triple, technique of classified, space ads,

SCORING YOUR TEST ANSWERS

Score five points for every Yes answer and zero for each No answer. Then add your total and place your score in this blank: _____.

Score	Evaluation
90 to 100	Great! This score means you are a highly ambitious person. Such ambition may well propel you to great levels of success.
80 to 90	This is a good level of ambition and still enough to take you a good way down the fast track to success. You can, however, raise this degree of ambition still higher.
70 to 80	This indicates a fair degree of ambition. You are probably somewhat limited in what you may attain, unless you are able to increase the amount of ambition you possess.
60 to 70	This score shows you are lacking in enough ambition. This might well be what is holding you back. Strive to get more ambition going for you.
50 to 60	You're out of the ball game. You should start at once to try to become a more ambitious person.

and/or direct mail. Once you've found out, you can try a similar method of advertising your own business.

Are Their Products or Services Attractive, Quality Offers?

I used to use the services of some small, out-of-town, mail-order printing companies. Most of them did fairly good work, but I occasionally found that some of the printing I ordered (circulars, sales letters, or order forms) arrived with smudges, torn corners, or other mistakes. When that happened, I asked that particular company to redo the work, or I simply never sent it another order.

The only way for you to find out if your competition's quality measures up to your own is to order some of their products and look them over. This can be of invaluable help to you in learning how you can beat your competition, whether your own product is superior or inferior to theirs, and how you might upgrade your own product.

Do Their Ads Use Color?

Do your competition's sales literature and advertisements use color, or are they simply black ink on white paper? The use of two or more colors is more attention-getting and attractive to prospects and usually brings in a larger number of orders than does black and white copy.

Do Your Competitors' Products Lend Themselves to Repeat Sales?

One of the best ways to grow and succeed in mail-order is to offer products or services by mail that lend themselves to repeat sales. Try to come up with a product that customers will buy again and again. That is a sure-fire way to substantial profits in the business.

Do Your Competitors' Sales Letters Include an Order Form as Part of the Letter or Is the Form Separate?

Generally speaking, you will usually receive more orders if you use a separate order form. It does save, however, on your printing cost to make the order form part of your sales letter. You can test both routes for yourself to see which one brings the most orders. Some mail-order companies use both methods for their various products.

THE HARD-LUCK, RAGS-TO-RICHES FORMULA

A number of the mail-order companies currently in business make use of a basic hard-luck, rags-to-riches ploy to sell their product or item. In my opinion, this formula has been milked to death, and I'm sure it's losing or has already lost some of its effectiveness. This sudden-riches formula often appears in "opportunity" magazines that offer do-it-yourself plans, programs, and systems for generating a larger income. The formula can clearly be seen in the large space ads that tell the reader a sad story (with a happy ending), using stock phrases and revelations like those in the following paraphrased lines:

- "I was at the end of my financial rope and desperate beyond belief. Then an incredible idea flashed across my mind."
- "That day I learned from my wife's best friend an amazing money secret that has completely turned my life . . . and my bank account . . . around."
- "This old-timer related his money plan to me on the spot, and I put it into effect the very next day. I couldn't believe how easy it was to make big money."
- "I kicked around from job to job feeling more and more sorry for myself all the time. My hope of attaining the American Dream was just whistling in the dark. Then, as if by divine guidance, I stumbled across a money-making system that I at first thought was far too good to be true. It proved me wrong. It was much better than all my hopes."
- "I'm about to reveal the most remarkable system you've ever seen or heard about. It can make you rich in just 60 days."
- "I had a lifetime of unfulfilled dreams. But what suddenly came into my life was a simple, but awesome, answer to all my financial problems."
- "You may be wondering why, if this program is so good, I'm willing to share it. One reason is because I'm a nice guy."
- "This system isn't just unique—it's fantastic!"
- "My method will show you how to get rich using credit cards . . . even if you have bad credit and not a single card to your name."
- "If you would like to make a year's income in one month, then here's your chance to get started."

Now tell me this: How can so many prospects be so stupid as to fall for these con-artist techniques? But they do. Thousands of people send in orders for these plans. Some of them reportedly work, though not as well as the ads claim they do. Many others, however, are complete duds that sound great when you read the ads but that, when you try them, simply fall apart.

Even some of the programs that can produce money have problems: They're too far-fetched, inconvenient, or simply very difficult to put into action. So why, please tell me, do they sell? The answer, again, is in the ads, which make the plans and programs sound like

- A sure thing
- A no-fail route to success
- A ticket to the big time
- An "open sesame" to millionaire status
- A shuttle to financial independence, a mansion of your own, and a garage full of Rolls-Royces

Why do people fall for these pipe dreams? Because their hopes are much larger than their brains. They live in a world of perpetual hope. But I'll tell you something loud and clear, and please realize that the next sentence is screaming out at you: You can take this formula and run with it, use it in your mail-order business, and maybe become rich from the money these dreamers send you.

Frankly, I'd rather not get rich by fleecing people out of $10.00 and $20.00 bills (or larger ones, not counting the postage and handling fees that the ads usually ask for). I want to be able to sleep well when each night comes.

I've always personally believed in treating others as I would like to be treated. I do my best to live by this philosophy. You can call it ethics, integrity, fair play, or whatever you like. My mail-order philosphy can be summed up this way: What good is having a lot of money if you can't come by it ethically, honestly, and by offering something of honest-to-God value? That's the way I feel and the way I try to run my own business.

Now look at the other side of the picture. Let's say you come up with a terrific money-making plan. I mean something that doesn't just sound good but that truly, really works. If that's the case, feel free to run the strongest, most dynamic ad you can create. Look at the reasons this route is so much better:

- You give each buyer honest value for his or her money.
- You stimulate buyers' hopes and may even bring them closer to their dreams because your plan or product *really* does what your ad says it will.
- You build a quality reputation for your mail-order company.
- You win repeat sales because your satisfied customers tell their friends, who in turn tell their friends. Those who ordered once will buy other products and offers from you.
- You run your company according to the industry's highest standards.
- You have pride in your offers and in your company.
- You reap handsome profits and build a substantial list of happy customers.
- You can sleep well at night.

ROUND-UP REPORTS ON THE BEST PLANS AND PROGRAMS

A fairly new way (at this writing) to make money in mail-order has emerged in the last year or so. This is to offer a round-robin report on ten or 20 of the get-rich-quick plans currently being advertised. One firm is doing this quite successfully, charging $39.95 for a subscription to its newsletter service. This newsletter-service company buys, researches, and tests the wealth-producing plans. It then reports on which plans are workable, which have too many problems or are too far-out, and which ones are complete duds.

Within a week, or even less time, you could put together such a report of your own. You would have to buy some of the programs to discover what they are, and you would have to test them. Then you could simply report your findings in a 10- or 20-page booklet. You could ask $10.00 or more for your booklet, selling it directly from ads or using the inquiry-and-follow-up method. Some companies that do this use full- and half-page ads to sell their research reports, but you could start more slowly with small ads and then gradually work up to good-sized space ads. I know this idea would make money for you

A MASTER PLAN FOR YOUR SUCCESS

Planning is a track to run on, a series of steps that you devise, work up, and apply to reach a certain objective. "Plan your work, and work your plan" is an often-heard rule, but the best plan in the world is no good unless it is put into action.

1. Set a planning period in your schedule at least once or twice a week. Decide how much time you'll devote to planning, whether one or several hours a week. Some people spend an hour every day on planning. A one-hour session a week should be the absolute minimum.

2. Write out the goals you wish to achieve. Be specific as to what you mean to accomplish. Set both large and small goals; smaller goals have a way of leading to larger ones.

3. Look over your goal list each time you have a planning session. It's also good to think about your next goal for at least a few minutes every day.

4. Do not let anything or anyone interfere with your planning periods. Your future may well depend on them.

5. Determine the new ideas and steps you can apply to move closer to your objective. Do this during each planning period.

6. Strive to gain more self-confidence. There is no doubt that when you increase your confidence, you automatically enlarge your chances for success.

W. Clement Stone, the Chicago insurance tycoon, had enough confidence in himself as a youth to start his own insurance company. He used his savings of $100 to launch his agency. He also had confidence that he could find good salespeople to join his new company. By 1930, a thousand agents were working for him, selling insurance all over America.

Stone's confidence paid off big. His company, Combined Insurance of America, became one of the most successful and respected firms in the insurance industry.

---

because I continue to see a lot of ads offering information on money-making systems.

So I've just given you another possible product for your mail-order company to sell. And you got it for free (or for the cost of this book). Your greatest expenses in getting this idea underway would be the ad costs and the cost of buying a selection of different money-making plans. If you can summarize your information in a few pages, the cost of making copies of your report should be very reasonable. Good luck if you decide to go with this idea.

THE CLEVER USE OF EMOTIONAL APPEALS

Famous author F. Scott Fitzgerald once said he would never even start a new short story unless there were an emotion closely involved in the story. The same thing could be said for good mail-order ads. The strongest ads cleverly play on people's wishes and make specific appeals to people's emotions.

The potential buyers you want to reach have a lot of desires. They want more money, recognition and praise, more creative ability, leisure time, self-esteem, appreciation, more fulfillment in their work, a chance to travel more, a nicer home or apartment, to be more attractive to the opposite sex, and quite a few other things as well.

To motivate your prospects to send you an order, you must stimulate these desires. You must relate whatever you're selling to the wishes of your potential buyers. If your offer does not fulfill one or more of these wants, the job of selling it will be extremely difficult.

Just about everyone wants a larger income, which is why so many money-making systems are advertised. This desire is constantly being catered to by many mail-order companies. Never forget that money-making plans are some of the hottest items in the world of mail-order. Real estate plans, money-broker businesses, finder's-fee setups, and similar products are mainly meant to do one thing for prospects: increase their money supply. If they are advertised even halfway effectively, they have an excellent chance of selling well.

Let's take a closer look at some of the appeals being used by many of today's mail-order companies.

1. Consider the appeal used in a full-page ad with the following headline:

Headline: Just Sit Back, Relax, and Let the Money Roll in!

The headline was preceded by this question: "Want to earn an extra $200–$500 a week spare time . . . with little effort?" The item being sold was an employment opportunity as an "art creations" representative. The offer would obviously appeal to many who read the ad. Who wouldn't like to earn $200 to $500 extra every week without much effort?

Notice that most advertisements for job opportunities no longer use the word "selling" or "sales." The words now being used are "representative" or "account executive" or "distributor." But what these jobs boil down to is sales.

2. Here is a good example of an ad that appeals to the desire to save money. At the same time, the ad tugs at the reader's curiosity to know more:

Headline: Every $1,000,000 System Revealed

In the body copy of the ad, the advertiser states that the buyer of the information "will save $495 on one money-making system alone." Some 50 different plans and programs are offered in the report.

3. The stopper in the following ad is the word "free." This magic word automatically locks in the interest of prospects and makes them want to know more. Their curiosity is stimulated to see what it's all about.

Headline: Yours Free! Complete information on the easiest big money you'll ever make in your life!

4. Here's a headline for a plan to make money with credit cards. Several similar plans are currently on the market.

Headline: You can make credit cards pay . . . regardless of your credit history!!

5. Here's an ad that ties in with a profession and therefore makes the program sounds classier than some of the others:

Headline: Become a Part of the Multi-Billion Dollar Legal Profession
Subhead: Starting with no experience or education, you can

get your share of the billions of dollars our judicial system holds for you.

To see if a prospective buyer "qualifies" for the legal-profession plan, the ad uses a ten-question test. The quiz asks only questions that would bring a "yes" from any reader. Here's one example: "Would you like to have $50,000 in the bank?"

6. Look at the very strong appeals to desire and curiosity in the following ad:

Headline: Get Paid for Wrapping Presents
Partial subhead: The secret is out! Now you can earn $50,000, $100,000, $200,000 or more annually by wrapping presents for pay.

Many prospects will find themselves driven to respond to the above ad. The curiosity factor is very strong here. Prospects will want to know what the plan is and how that much money can really be made by wrapping gifts. (The ad, however, would not move me personally to take action. I can't wrap presents. Not well, I mean. I do a lousy job of wrapping. Always have. So I guess that would let me out of the big money promised by the ad's subhead, even if it really is true.)

7. Consider the appeal in the following two-inch display ad:

Headline: Now You Can Have Your Own $5,000 Line of Credit
In body of ad: The company [name] "offers you the things you want (TVs, cameras, household items, beautiful gifts, etc."

8. I would say the curiosity appeal of the following ad is much stronger than its appeal to the prospect's desires.

Headline: Get Paid for Doing Basic Research
Subhead: You can earn $10.00 to $20.00 per hour, or more, doing simple research in the comfort of your own home.

THE BONUS AND P.S. DOUBLE WHAMMY

Glance through the ads in leading mail-order publications, and you'll usually see the clever, strategic use of two psychological "extras" that can definitely increase the number of orders you receive. These extras are the "bonus" and the "P.S." If you're not using these in your advertising, you're losing two chances to further persuade and convince your prospects to send you their orders.

Many investment newsletters make very effective use of the bonus and the P.S. One direct-mail sales letter I recently received offered a whopping *seven* free bonus extras for anyone who subscribed for two or more years. For a one-year subscription to the newsletter, the number of bonus extras offered dropped to three, but that was still enough to make me think seriously of sending in an order.

Incentive Is the Name of the Game

Some advertisers come up with such enticing bonuses that a lot of the customers who send in orders are actually buying the lead item in order to get the bonus. It happens all the time. Sometimes orders will be accompanied by little notes that say, "Be sure to send my bonus." So the more attractive your bonus item is, the stronger the incentive will be for prospects to order your main product.

When you really think about it, to run a mail-order company is to be in the commercial business. Copywriters are business people. What they bring to the industry is their knowledge of selling, merchandise, and general business procedures. Copywriting is persuasion. The headline and body copy of an ad are of course important, but the addition of a free bonus is smart business. An attractive bonus offer in your ad or sales letter can work like a magnet, drawing in many additional orders.

The more alluring your product and bonus sound, the more likely a prospect will be to send you an order. Consider the following bonus offers:

> *Bonus example:* If you are one of the first 150 "early birds"
> this month, you will receive a special bonus system that
> may add up to $2,000 weekly to your gross income.

Notice how the following bonus is made to tie in with a
guarantee:

> *Bonus example:* My unique program is so simple and easy to
> use that anyone who follows my simple instructions and
> doesn't earn in excess of $100,000 in 90 days will receive
> from me a complete refund of not 100 percent, but 200
> percent.

Such bonuses sound great, as well as too good to be true.
But they can do a lot to get prospects over their indecision and
convince them to send in orders.

The Case for a P.S.

Did you know what element of an ad or sales letter is read most
often, after the headline? The answer is the P.S., if one appears.
Remember the hit song "P.S., I Love You"? It was an enormous
success and was recorded by many of the leading singers of that
era. What worked well on record also works effectively in ads
and sales literature. Some advertisers fail to use a P.S., and they
miss out on a final chance to say something that might help
clinch an order. You do see a lot of P.S. use in direct-mail sales
letters. I urge you always to use a P.S. in your own sales letters.
You should consider using a P.S., if it seems appropriate and
you have enough space, in your display ads, too.

You can use a P.S. to wrap up the ad or to summarize again
the number-one reason for your prospect to act without delay.
You can also use it to say that you hope the reader is not going
to pass up the chance to see your plan, program, system, or
other offer. Added to the other selling tools, the P.S. forms an
arsenal of strong reasons for your prospects to buy from you.
But remember that some types of P.S. extras are stronger and
more enticing than others.

ELEMENTS OF A CLASSIFIED AD

1. Lead or headline: Come up with one word or several that grab the reader's attention.
2. Promise: Name some benefit the product offers.
3. Description: Describe the product itself.
4. Guarantee: Push the prospective customer into action with a no-risk offer.

Large space ads do not always use a P.S., but most direct-mail sales letters make very effective use of it. Here is an example taken from a direct marketer of insurance products:

P.S.: You can save even more by paying on an annual basis. This way, you get 12 full months of protection for only 11 times your monthly premium. So you save one month's premium. If you have any questions or need assistance, call us toll-free.

Here is another example of a P.S., this one taken from a direct-mail sales letter from The National Investment Challenge:

P.S.: REMEMBER, up for grabs is over $100,000 in cash and prizes in this NEW, EXCITING and FUN competition called The National Investment Challenge.

Remember that headlines and P.S. lines are the most often read elements of ads and direct-mail sales letters. Use strong ones.

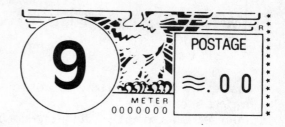

Your Vision and Leadership Set the Pace

By the time you read these words, we'll be into the 1990s. As the decade unfolds, you'll need to keep two basic truths in mind. One is simply that you have a right to be successful—especially if you're willing to pay the price of success by giving your company strong leadership, setting the pace in planning, persistence, and sacrifice. The second truth is that the seeds of success—or greater success—already lie within you.

Think of Niagara Falls. The waterfall consists of two cataracts, the Horseshoe Falls and the American Falls. Some 84 million gallons of water flow over the Horseshoe Falls every minute. The waters of Niagara are one of the world's greatest sources of hydroelectric power. There is a great power within you, too. Learn how to tap the marvelous powers of your own subconscious mind, and you may reach a level of mail-order success beyond your wildest dreams.

THE UNKNOWN FACTOR

Something special lies beyond the qualities and traits most people exercise and apply daily to achieve a healthy degree of success. I call it the "unknown factor," or "X-plus." Some prefer to think of it as guidance or direction from the subconscious mind. Others call it "that certain something." There is no doubt, however, that the following characteristics are true of X-plus:

- X-plus makes a person move out in front and go to the top of his or her vocation or profession.
- X-plus is something extra, deep within, that drives a person to get ahead.

In other words, X-plus is that unknown factor that causes a person to become a champion. Those who have it somehow know it, although they may call it something else. It was this X-plus quality that enabled Frank Bettger, author of *How I Raised Myself from Failure to Success in Selling*, to rise from being just another salesman to the level of a champion. Bettger worked out a system for coordinating and applying positive sales techniques such as learning to listen, remembering names, enthusiasm, using questions, "prospecting," effectively closing a sale, and so on. What was it that gave Bettger the power to do this? Call it skill, courage, or determination—it was the fuel-power that changed his selling career and life.

At the tender age of ten, George S. Patton announced his serious intention to become a great soldier and general. From the time he chose his objective as a boy in California, he never wavered. As a young cadet at West Point, the future general was in danger of being dropped from the academy for failing first-year mathematics. Instead he went through the first, tough year a second time, sparing no effort to earn rank and honors.

Patton attained his life goal. At Bastogne, Belgium, where Hitler's hopes during World War II really ended, Patton's Third Army moved farther in less time, engaging more enemy divisions, than any other army in the history of the United States.

Patton would not yield and did not believe in giving up. His constant command was "Attack . . . attack!" He knew even at the start of his amazing career that he could and would attain his goal. He had a white-hot desire to become a great general, and that is exactly what he achieved. Patton certainly drew on the reservoir of X-plus within him.

THE STUFF OF CHAMPIONS

Most of us fall by the wayside, especially if the going gets tough. But the champion says, "When the going gets tough, the tough get going." The champion constantly reaches out for more. A champion is willing to keep getting up, no matter how many times he or she may be knocked down. The spirit of a genius is stirring in the champion's soul, for experts have proven that genius is largely the courage to keep trying, along with plain hard work.

Somehow, the X-plus quality enables budding champions to hear the sound of a distant drum. That drumroll says they can—and will—make it, even before they try. It lets them know they will make a unique mark in the world.

TAKE A TIP FROM BILLIONAIRE HOWARD HUGHES

One of the best examples of the importance of vision is the case of billionaire Howard Hughes. Hughes had the ability to project his sights into the future and realize a coming trend ahead of time. Some years before the jet age arrived, Hughes saw it coming and bought a lot of TWA stock. When the age of jet travel dawned, Hughes made a fortune. It was this initial fortune that Hughes parlayed into his well-known billions.

So why not take a tip from Howard Hughes and try to develop your vision while building your mail-order company and your own distinctive line of products and services? To be able to see what lies ahead is an unusual ability and very valuable. There are some clues as to what the future of mail-order holds, and we'll look at them in the final chapter of this book.

BACK UP YOUR RIGHT TO SUCCESS

A majority of people feel they have a right to be successful. But what brings results is backing up that right with action. Old saying or not, the need to "take the bull by the horns" is as true now as ever.

"Hold on with a bulldog grip, and chew and choke as much as possible." Those were the words Abraham Lincoln used in a telegram he sent to General Ulysses S. Grant during the siege of Petersburg, Virginia. To phrase the idea another way, you must stay committed to the success you want and take some action toward getting it every day. When tycoon J. Paul Getty was starting his career back in 1915, he no doubt thought he had a right to be successful. But he knew he couldn't count on that alone. He had to take steps toward the success he wanted. So, even in his first venture, Getty showed the imagination and decisiveness that made his name and life a legend. Had he not made his vast fortune in oil, I believe he could have gotten very rich as a mail-order entrepreneur.

Getty possessed only $500 to use in bidding for his first oil lease. He correctly figured that other bidders would offer higher amounts, so he engaged a bank to do his bidding for him. As soon as his competitors saw the name of the bank listed as one of the bidders, they became discouraged since they believed the bank would easily outbid them. Getty got the lease, which he sold. The lease had oil, as he had thought, and Getty's profit in the deal was $39,000. His career continued to boom from that point forward.

When the great athlete Jim Thorpe went to the 1912 Olympics in Sweden, he carried with him much more than the belief that he had the right to be successful. He also took along a dominating will to succeed. Thorpe, winner of two events at that Olympics, achieved a total point-score that stood unbroken for 20 years. In 1912, no one else could even come close to his record. In addition to the honors and many awards Thorpe won, the King of Sweden said these words to him personally: "Sir, you are the greatest athlete in the world." The main reasons Thorpe was victorious were his confidence in himself and his will to succeed.

Do you have this kind of will to succeed in mail-order? If you do, there will be no stopping you, provided you sell products and services people want. What about confidence? Do you have enough confidence in yourself and your company to blaze a trail to new levels of profits and success? Match confidence and the will to win, and you've got a powerful combination.

Yes, the basic right to be successful is yours. But to make the success you seek become a reality, more is needed. By backing up your right to be successful with commitment, a healthy amount of X-plus, action, vision, and a will to succeed, you can develop all the fuel power needed to be victorious.

PAY OFF ALL YOUR DEBTS PROMPTLY

Before you take action to expand your mail-order company by adding new offers to your line, or even if you're just getting your own company launched, I strongly recommend that you pay off all your debts. A number of people are eventually forced to leave the business because of debt. They develop reputations for not paying bills or for being very slow to pay. Some let bills stack up for so long that they reach the point where the debt can't possibly be paid.

I urge you to form the following habits. They are signs of a solid, reputable, and professional mail-order company:

1. Pay all bills as quickly as possible. Doing so will help you build an excellent credit record fast.
2. Companies that pay bills promptly and continually develop solid reputations in the industry. Make it a point to have the check in the mail whenever you say it is. Pay the printers you work with promptly. The same goes for the advertising you run. Pay for it either up front or as soon as possible.
3. If you use an in-house ad agency (meaning one you set up in order to get the 15 percent discount offered to ad agencies by many magazines and newspapers), you should open a separate checking account in the agency's name. Pay for all ad insertions out of that account. The mail-order sections of some newspapers may not allow

you this discount, but most leading mail-order magazines will. They want your advertising dollars.

4. Use professional-looking letterhead stationery for both your main company and your ad agency. You can't do any real business without a good letterhead.

5. Respond immediately to all refund requests. Some mail-order firms offer a 14-, 30-, or 90-day guarantee. Other companies extend the refund period to six months. One successful company made it a practice to send a refund to any customer who requested it for up to a year after the purchase. Still other mail-order companies put no time limits at all on their guarantees.

Anyone who is in debt would be foolish to start a mail-order company or attempt to expand an existing one. It's far better to wait until your debts are paid. Then you can launch or expand your company in the full knowledge that the profits will be yours to keep or to plow back into your business.

Remember, too, that among the hottest selling mail-order items, in recent years, have been manuals and books on how to get out of debt. As long as the United States—and the world, for that matter—has so many people in debt, there will be a considerable market for such guidance. Maybe your own system for getting out of debt would be profitable if you were to market it. Or perhaps you've devised a plan to avoid getting into debt in the first place. So there's another offer idea for your company. You might do well with it and make some additional profits.

SUCCESS WITH THE "BIG THREE"

To a large degree, the success you seek in mail-order lies within you. As we've seen, a number of personal qualities are vital for success. Some people are more aware of these success motivators than others. I want you now to focus your attention on three of them: persistence, drive, and what I call "working smart," or efficiency. Begin to think of these three dynamics as the three *musts* for success. They can certainly do a lot to increase your mail-order profits and success.

Persistence

A clear way to think about persistence is to see it simply as the art of not giving up. One day during World War II, Winston Churchill was visiting Harrow School in England. He strolled through the classrooms, and everyone thought that he would say something cheerful to the children. But the thought of the Nazis and all they were doing so enraged the great leader that he suddenly dashed his cane on an empty desk, crying: "Never give up! Never never never never never never!"

Persistence is power. It is actually more important than talent. In the famous boxing match between Jim Corbett and then-champion John L. Sullivan held in New Orleans on September 7, 1892, Corbett started to dodge Sullivan at the sound of the first bell. Sullivan roared for Corbett to "come in and fight," but the challenger refused. For 20 rounds, Corbett continued to dodge Sullivan until he realized that his opponent was ready for the kill. His entire strategy had been to avoid Sullivan's rushes while getting in counterpunches. Corbett knocked the champion out in the twenty-first round. "Gentleman" Jim Corbett, as he was called, often gave out his advice for more successful living: "When you're weary from trying, don't quit; fight one more round. That one more round may make all the difference and bring you success."

Drive

Drive is a vital tool to have in your success kit. It is quite clear that some people have the ability to muster much more of this quality than others. Big success in mail-order takes a lot of careful planning, but also the drive to see that all those plans are coordinated and running smoothly.

Maybe the secret of drive is in liking your work. If you like the mail-order business, you will enjoy all the phases of the work. Happy is the man or woman who enjoys his or her work, for then functioning in the daily job becomes like play or sport. It's far easier to summon energy and drive if you're doing work that interests, excites, and challenges you.

"Working Smart" (Efficiency)

A big part of being smarter about your work means planning for the future. Whatever you hope to achieve in the years ahead, you will find the following guidelines helpful. Use them as a handy reference to enable yourself to get more done in less time and to work with more overall efficiency.

1. Set a regular time each day or week when you do nothing else but plan for the weeks and months ahead. Some executives plan their entire year in advance, in a general way.
2. Check your goal list every time you have a planning session. Cross out the goals you have achieved and substitute new ones. Think often about the next goal on your list. And always keep in mind that the little goals you attain have a way of leading to the realization of large ones.
3. Work toward both short- and long-range goals at all times. Know where you would like to be five years from now, or beyond, and how you intend to get there.
4. Write out a brief evaluation report each quarter on how you seem to be doing. If the results look poor, don't get discouraged or give up. Keep your planning session each time. Believe that the results will improve, and you will find that they usually do.

SUCCESS AND GOOD FORTUNE FAVOR THE BOLD

There are basically two types of people in this world. First, there are those who either cannot or will not think and act more boldly. Many of them try, but they do not seem to be able to sustain bold thinking and action long enough for good things to happen for them. So what does happen? Millions of such people just drift through their best and most vibrant years. The parade of life and success passes them by.

The other type of person is the man or woman who discovers the crucial importance of boldness and starts thinking and acting more boldly every day. Things begin to happen for this type of person after a period of applying this bold form of action and thought.

How do you know how far you can go in the mail-order business? How do you know what you can achieve and accomplish in the world, unless you are giving it all you've got? Boldness is more than just simply trying; it's the act of daring to do something great, the act of placing yourself and your ideas where you (and they) can rise to a higher level of success and achievement in the world.

Remember, your own vision and leadership will set the pace for your company's growth and success. Make no small plans. Reach for the top. Chart your course for ever-higher vistas of mail-order profits. They're out there waiting for you.

Collaborating With Other Mail-Order People

A great many mail-order companies are run by just one person, but husband-and-wife combinations sometimes do very well. It's always possible to team up with a friend, neighbor, relative, or family member. There's no doubt that collaboration in business can work. But you should be careful whom you decide to cast your lot with. It reminds me of the advice a top New York literary agent once gave to writers: ''Signing on with an agent is, in a way, like getting married. That's why it's better to meet and talk person-to-person to any agent you're considering. You need to be careful so you'll make the right marriage.''

If and when the question, and possibility, of collaboration comes up for you, here are some steps you should take:

1. Get any agreements regarding your collaboration in writing. If you have the contract in writing, you'll have a lot more going for you in any dispute that may arise.

2. Be sure to date any agreement forms, and both you and your collaborator should sign them.
3. If you and your partner pool your money resources to start or expand a mail-order company, be sure to spell out how much each of you contributed in a clear, written statement. Be sure your statement gives the percentage of profits each of you is to earn.

Say, for example, that during your collaboration period you together come up with a terrific product or service, and the two of you agree to share equally in launching and promoting it and in any profits it brings. That's fine. But what happens if you and your collaborator split up and your ex-partner believes he or she still deserves a full half-share of that item's earnings? Unless you have a prior agreement, this could become a serious legal problem.

It could also happen the other way around. Say that your collaborator originates a marvelous offer and that it does very well for your company, spinning off profits year after year. Then later, after your partnership has broken up, your collaborator believes that he or she is the sole owner of the item, since he or she was its creator. Your former partner may want to cut you off from sharing in the item's profits any longer. In fact, he or she could open a competing mail-order company, fully believing that only he or she can legitimately sell the item. To protect both of your rights, you need to have the basic terms of your partnership stated in a legally binding document. Some collaborators have a formal partnership agreement drawn up in order to avoid any future problems.

If both you and your partner leave the mail-order industry, dissolving your company, there should be a clause or statement to the effect that, after all bills are paid, you will share equally in any remaining assets.

A lawyer can answer any specific questions you may have. And you need not concern yourself about this matter unless you expect to enter into a collaborative relationship. The thing I want you to remember is that, while many partnerships are started and run on nothing more than a handshake, it's usually safer to put at least the basic terms of your partnership into writing. This will obviously be all the more vital should your mail-order company skyrocket and take in a great deal of money.

THE URGE TO MERGE

Big corporations have no monopoly on the desire to team up with other companies. This ''urge to merge'' is also felt in the mail-order industry, though to a more limited degree.

If the idea of collaboration intrigues you, try to get to know other mail-order operators. You may well come across a kindred spirit who shares your vision, your hopes for the future, and your enthusiasm, interest, and love for the mail-order business. Here are some ways you might explore to find someone to collaborate with or at least to meet others in the industry, from among whom you might select a future collaborator:

- Attend conferences, seminars, or conventions on advertising, direct marketing, motivational research, and new product development.
- Watch the trade papers and leading mail-order publications for feature articles about successful mail-order companies and entrepreneurs. Then contact those people by mail, telephone, or even in person.
- Run an ad or series of ads in which you try to reach someone already in the business (and preferably doing well) who might be interested in a merger with your company.
- Convince a friend of yours to join you in a mail-order company partnership. Try to pick someone with whom you get along well and who seems to have an interest in advertising and the mail-order industry.

PROS AND CONS OF USING DISTRIBUTORS

Some mail-order operators decide at one point or another to use distributors to get their advertising circulars and offers into the hands of more potential buyers. The attractive thing about using distributors is the time they can save you. If you have a number of distributors sending out your circulars, you can reach more prospects in less time, and with less strain on you.

Advantages of Using Distributors

As your company grows, you just may not have the time to sit down and personally stuff 5,000, 25,000, or however many envelopes. So let's look at the major advantages of using distributors:

1. Distributors save you time.
2. Many distributors offer reasonable rates for sending out your circulars and ad offers.
3. You suffer less strain, and you are given the chance to focus on other aspects of your business.
4. Using distributors makes it easier to test your circulars and offers in different sections of the country.
5. Distributors often offer bargain rates to print and mail circulars. This can often lower your printing and postage costs considerably.

Disadvantages of Using Distributors

There are also some disadvantages in working with distributors. Here are a few:

1. Some distributors will include your circular in a pack containing seven or eight others. This greatly reduces the prospect's attention and focus on your offer.

2. Many distributors expect a share or ''split'' of orders received. They may expect, for example, to keep $5.00 out of a product cost of $10.00. Different distributors make different kinds of split arrangements.

3. There are some small mail-order companies that seem to spend all their time circulating their offers to other mail-order firms. Some of them publish monthly magazines with names like *Mail-Order Bulletin*. A lot of ads for distributors appear in these lesser-known publications. Be careful. I followed through on a number of such ads years ago with poor results. I believe

it's best to stick to the leading publications in the industry and to avoid these others.

4. You may have no assurance that your circulars and offer ads are really mailed by distributors. Some of them simply don't report back or respond. I recently sent orders to have some circulars printed and mailed by two small print-and-mail companies which agreed to do it for a set price. I asked for confirmations in both cases. I have yet to hear from them. I sent them checks, but they didn't even have the basic business courtesy of acknowledging my orders and confirming that my circulars were mailed. While these were print-and-mail firms, some so-called reliable distributors operate in the same way. I recommend that you deal with proven, reliable companies and mail-order publications for the best results, more integrity and honesty, and overall professionalism. Remember, anybody can hang out a shingle and say he or she is in the mail-order business. Unfortunately, some seem to have the idea that's all they need.

RIGHT AND WRONG TIMES TO COLLABORATE

If you believe you can make it on your own in mail-order and build your company up yourself, you shouldn't even consider collaboration. If your company is already underway and you're simply eager to expand, keep the following points in mind:

1. You might be far better off expanding your company on your own, even though it might take more time to do so.
2. If you have any reservations at all about a possible collaboration, this is the wrong time to go ahead.
3. If you and your collaborator get along well, agree on the basics of the business, and all signals seem to point to a promising merger, then this could be the right time to collaborate. Make sure, though, that you have a plan of definite, specific goals for your new partnership to achieve.

Use your common sense. If a collaboration looks a bit risky to you, or you're just not sure about it, don't risk what you've already accomplished. The wrong kind of partner might talk you into some new item or advertising strategy that could prove to be a disaster.

Remember, the number-one reason most new businesses fail is lack of knowledge about how to run a business efficiently. You need to see a number of strong, solid reasons why you should collaborate. If they just aren't there, don't let yourself be talked into something you might regret.

It's nice not to have to share the profits of your business with someone else. If you feel you can do it on your own, then by all means go ahead by yourself. You may be a lot happier and richer for it down the road. Many one-person mail-order firms do very well, and their operators have a lot of fun, too. Many don't wish to get too big. They prefer to stay a medium size or smaller. And many such people even hold down 40-hour-a-week jobs, running their mail-order companies on a part-time basis.

By going it alone, you may save yourself a lot of trouble and time. In the final analysis, there's nothing like running your own show. You're the boss, the top gun, the number-one decision maker. By keeping full control of your company and its future, you always know where you're going.

POSTAGE

$\approx$. 0 0

METER
0000000

Finding the Money to Build Your Business

To develop and expand your mail-order company, you need to plan, coordinate, and put into action a basic strategy. This strategy should be based on a number of sound ways to increase your company's profits. In this chapter, we will look at a number of key ways to put such a strategy in place.

RUN YOUR BEST-PULLING ADS IN MORE PUBLICATIONS

As you probably know, pyramid schemes and chain letters are illegal. But pyramiding your profits is entirely legal and the very way many well-known names in mail-order achieved their great success.

Pyramiding your profits is an easy concept to understand and apply. What you do is simply to take the profits from two, six, or a dozen (or more) ads you run and plow those profits back into additional advertising. In other words, you don't bank your profits. Not yet. You pay your expenses and advertising costs up front and then, if there are any profits, you immediately place more ads in more publications.

Joe Karbo, the mail-order genius who developed the ad called "The Lazy Man's Way to Riches," made this method work for him. It can work for you if your ads are strong and you have a sound product or service to offer.

Once the ads you run are bringing in a consistent profit and you feel the time is right to expand your company and the volume of business you are doing, you will find it helpful to make a list of all the leading mail-order publications. Then plan your advertising campaign to pyramid your profits. Say, for example, the first mail-order publications you put down on your list are the following:

> *Income Opportunities* (magazine)
> *Popular Mechanics* (magazine)
> *Opportunity* (magazine)
> *The Star* (weekly tabloid newspaper)

And say the profits of your classified ad in *Income Opportunities* amount to $400. Then you take that money and buy from one to four (that is, as many as the money will buy) additional classified ads to run in the next available issues of *Popular Mechanics*, *Opportunity*, and *The Star*.

The cost of these additional ads will determine whether you're able to run just one ad or more in the other three publications. You might, for example, be able to run several ads in two of the three publications. It all depends on how many words in length your ads are. If you can hold down the number of words in your ads, then it's possible for you to run the same, short ad in two different classified categories in each of the three other publications. The idea is to buy as many additional ads in as many other publications as your profits allow.

If you're using display, or space, ads instead of classifieds, you can use the same pyramiding strategy. Space ads are obviously more expensive than classifieds. By way of example, let's say one or two small display ads brought profits of several hundred dollars. You can take that money and buy one or two additional display ads. If the results prove to be about the same, your profits will then double or triple. Again, you take these profits and plow them back into five, six, or seven ads.

I'm sure you get the idea. Each time you realize profits from the ads you already have running, you put those profits to work for you at once in the form of more ads in other leading mail-order publications. If you're able to keep pyramiding your profits in this until you have ads running in dozens of publications, then your total profits can increase enormously. That is essentially the concept of profit pyramiding.

Bear in mind that it's possible some of your ads won't bring in a profit or enough of a profit to pay for additional ads. If that should happen, you should scratch the unproductive ads and stick with the ones that get you good results. Or try designing completely new ads, but test them before going ahead with a pyramiding-the-profits strategy.

In fact, the ads you initially use, before you start plowing profits back into more ads, have to be very strong, attention-grabbing, and magnetic: the kind of ads that will make potential buyers reach for their checkbooks. If those first ads don't bring in any profits, you'll simply have to go back to the drawing board, plan some stronger campaign, and then try again. Remember, though, that it's possible to rewrite an ineffective ad to make it much stronger.

A good way to try pyramiding your profits without risking too much is to limit the scheme to classified ads at first. If you do well using only classifieds, then you can try the same strategy in display ads. Realize up front that display ads will cost you considerably more money than classifieds, but will also return much larger profits to you, if your ads are winners. Once you've got a few tried-and-tested, winning display ads bringing in good profits, you're on your way to a small, medium, or giant-size fortune.

A word of warning is in order here. The strategy of pyramiding profits into more and more ads sounds simple and easy to do, but don't make the mistake of thinking it's duck soup. A lot of factors can affect your ads' results. Here are some of the leading ones:

- The time and season you run your ads
- The pulling quality, or lack of it, of your ads
- The asking price for your product or service

- Whether your objective is to sell directly from your ads or to use the inquiry-and-follow-up system
- Whether your competitors are making similar offers, and how your products or services compare with the competition's
- Which mail-order publications you choose to start with
- Whether you choose to work with classified or display ads
- The categories you select to run your ads under—Business Opportunities, Of-Interest-to-All, Books, or whatever

INVITE ONE OR MORE PARTNERS TO JOIN YOU

One way to raise money for your company's expansion is to make a partnership offer. You could run an ad for this in *The Wall Street Journal, Income Opportunities*, or one of the other leading mail-order publications. Even an ad run in your local newspaper could bring you some inquiries. It seems there are always some individuals with money out there interested in buying into a growing, successful company.

If you can get hold of a list of successful businesspeople in your region, you could propose your partnership to these people in a sales letter. Then you could meet personally with any who respond expressing interest.

Sometimes small or medium-size mail-order companies unite their resources, knowledge, experience, and customer lists to create a larger and more successful operation. You should regularly watch the ads that appear in well-known mail-order publications to see if any companies are seeking to merge with other firms. If you see such ads, you can respond and check them out, or you could run similar ads yourself.

Ads occasionally appear that offer lists of very rich Arab companies and individuals who might have interest in buying half-ownership (or a smaller percentage) of your company and joining you as either a silent or an active partner. But don't neglect American companies and entrepreneurs. There are people and firms in the United States that might be interested in joining you. Watch the Sunday classifieds sections of *The*

New York Times for any ads indicating interest in forming partnership deals.

In this era of mergers and acquisitions, you stand a better chance of finding one or more partners. But the present merger trend could fade in the months and years ahead.

"ANGELS" ARE LOOKING FOR GROWTH COMPANIES

Some of the better mailing-list sources may have special lists of "angels" interested in funding your company's expansion in return for a share in the profits. You could contact these mailing-list companies and ask for details on their most up-to-date lists of such "angels." You may have to pay a fairly high fee to rent such lists, but it might be well worth it if only a few— or one—of those "angels" decides to invest money in your company.

Such "angels" will ask to see specifics on your company's bottom line, profits, the product or service items you offer, and your expansion plans for the future. You will probably need to work up a presentation package to show your firm's history; your present customer list, expenses, profits; and how you intend to build your company. Some "angels" will ask for more information than others.

If you don't wish to go the mailing-list route in your search for "angels," I suggest you watch the big city newspapers, particularly their Sunday editions, for classified or display ads in which companies or individuals express interest in investing in growth companies. You yourself could run a series of ads in selected publications including big city Sunday newspapers. Here's an example of how such an ad might read:

> "Angel" Wanted for Investment in
> Growing Mail-Order Company!

You should be certain to include your address and company name so any responses will reach you. Strange as it may seem, I occasionally see ads with no company name, or where the address has apparently been left out.

TAKE A CHANCE ON BIG-RETURN INVESTMENTS

Perhaps your mail-order company is rolling along fairly well, and has been for some time, but you definitely want to expand it and go for larger profits. One course of action might be for you to take a chance on some big-return investments. Your investment ventures might be in one or more of the following areas:

- Stocks
- Real estate
- Mutual funds
- The Japanese stock market
- Commodities
- A sideline business that looks very promising for a big return

A Strategy for Sound Investing

Sound, shrewd investing might well be the best way to fund the future growth of your company. It might take you some time to realize large enough profits on your investments, but, if so, then you would simply have to delay expanding your mail-order company until you've raised the money you need. I'm not saying this is what you should do. That decision can only be made by you. But investing might well be the way to get the money for expansion. Perhaps you could put some of your mail-order company's profits into stock investments, but of course this would limit the amount you would be able to plow back into additional mail-order ads.

You naturally have to be willing to take chances to make progress in investing. Bernard Baruch, statesman and "Wizard of Wall Street," believed in taking chances in life, and he applied this philosophy to the art of investing. "There is no investment which doesn't involve some risk and is not something of a gamble," said Baruch. The key objective, as Baruch saw it, is to "try to reduce the element of risk in whatever you undertake. . . . The true speculator is one who observes the future and acts before it occurs."

Baruch clearly believed that human reactions to economic forces and changing events drive stock prices up or down. Because they are human, stock owners *react*. Some are too quick to panic and sell. Others are too calm and overconfident, and hold onto stocks longer than they should.

A Code for Profitable Investing

Bernard Baruch's advice for smart investing is still used by many people today. His guidelines can help you to realize large profits on your investments, and then you can use your accumulated profits to expand your mail-order business. Here is a code of advice, adapted from Baruch's guidelines for wise investing:

1. Before you buy a stock, find out everything you can about the company. As a possible investor, you should compare the cash a company actually has on hand with its debts. Does the company make a product or offer a service that the public really wants or needs? Companies that are meeting real needs are much more likely to grow and prosper. Keep abreast of the things people must have or want to have. (Some of this advice, as you can see, can also help you in your mail-order business.)

2. Don't buy too many different stocks. It's better to have relatively few investments that can be watched carefully. How can an investor accurately watch a wide variety of stocks? Changes come quickly, and unless you have a trained staff of intelligent assistants to keep up with each stock, play it cool and limit the amount of stocks you buy.

3. Don't speculate unless you can make it a full-time job. The basic facts and latest information about companies must be constantly kept up with. This takes time. If you don't have the time to devote to a continual study of what is going on at different companies, it is wiser not to speculate. Baruch felt that to be done wisely, speculating must be a full-time endeavor.

In order to speculate full-time, you would of course have to put your mail-order company on hold. Or you could try to speculate part-time, realizing that you take a bigger risk by only devoting part of your attention to it.

4. Don't try to buy at the bottom and sell at the top. This

can't be done, except by liars. Baruch believed that it is much harder to know when to sell a stock than when to buy. "The sensible course, he wrote, "is to sell while the stock is still rising, or, if you've made a mistake, to admit it at once and take your loss." Many speculators find it tough on their egos to admit to themselves that they were wrong about a certain company. They like a given stock and cannot understand why it is on the skids. This forming of attachments to favorite stocks can be very costly.

5. Always keep a good part of your capital in a cash reserve. Never invest all your funds. By keeping a large reserve of cash, Baruch was in a position to "take advantage of unforseen opportunities."

6. Beware of barbers, beauticians, waiters, or anyone bringing gifts of "inside" information or tips. It is very easy for a speculator to fall prey to a worthless tip. What usually happens is that an investor lets emotions take over and crush his or her ability to reason. To speculate wisely and profitably calls for considerable reasoning ability and good judgment. By acting on something overheard or a "hot tip" about a stock, you can lose your shirt and more.

7. Learn how to take your losses quickly and cleanly. Don't expect to be right all the time. If you've made a mistake, cut your losses as quickly as possible. Baruch placed a lot of emphasis on this basic rule. An investor must accept the truth that there is no way one can be right all the time. Realize at the start that you are going to make mistakes. Every speculator-investor does. Just accept it and get out of a bad investment as soon as possible.

8. Study your tax position to know when you can sell to greatest advantage. Baruch periodically turned most of his holdings into cash and retired temporarily from the market. He found this practice to be a wise one. "I tried never to go into any speculation over my depth—beyond my financial ability to pay for any error of judgment," he said. This rule is also good advice for operating your mail-order company.

9. Make a periodic reappraisal of all your investments to see whether changing developments have altered their prospects. Many investors buy stocks for long-term growth, putting them away safely for long periods. It shows good judgment to look

them over from time to time with a view to whether recent changes have hurt their chances for growth. As Baruch repeatedly pointed out, "One cannot make an investment and take for granted that its worth will remain unchanged. Often something will shrink in value because of one discovery only to be given new economic life by another development."

10. Don't try to be a jack-of-all-investments. Stick to the field you know best. Baruch strongly criticized the many people who think they can do anything, "buy and sell stock, dabble in real estate, run a business, engage in politics—all at once." In his own experience, he found that few people can do more than one thing at a time and do it well.

To do well in investing you may find it necessary to cease operating your mail-order business. The investing advice above is presented only as a possible way to raise the money you need to expand your mail-order company. If it takes too much of your time, you may prefer to abandon your investing activity and focus again on mail-order. These decisions are up to you.

But remember, following the rules above can do much to increase your investment profits. Again, Baruch stressed over and over the vital importance of getting all the facts about a given situation before acting. Obtaining this information is a continuous job. "It requires eternal vigilance," as Baruch pointed out.

Here's another helpful point from the master of investment success: "The stock market does not determine the health of our economy. All it does is register the judgments of buyers and sellers on what business is like and what it will be like in the future. The stock market is the thermometer, not the fever."

Baruch limited his operations to only a few key areas. When he lost, he studied hard to find out why. "I always analyzed my losses to see where I'd made my mistakes," he said. You, too, must learn from your mistakes, which you are bound to make. Baruch was a keen student of history. He wrote, "If we but learn the lessons that shriek from the pages of history, there is no handicap that cannot be overcome by willpower, patience, and application. The future is actually bright with promise. The trend of civilization itself is always upward."

If and when you try investing as a means of raising money to expand your mail-order company, turn back to these guidelines and rules from Wall Street's wizard. They will work well for you just as they did for Baruch.

SOME SOURCES FOR BUSINESS LOANS AND EXPANSION CAPITAL

Here are some addresses of possible sources of loans and expansion money to build your company. Please bear in mind that addresses are subject to change. Also, I can make no assurance whatsoever that you will be able to obtain a loan. Every case is different. You should first write to the companies listed and ask for information.

1. Stocks and Securities
   One of the quickest ways to raise money is to sell any stocks you may own, provided you won't be taking a loss to do so.

2. Fidelcor Business Credit Corporation
   (offices in New York, Richmond, Chicago, Dallas, Los Angeles, Miami, Philadelphia, San Francisco)
   Present toll-free number: 1-800-343-3526

3. Englett's Department 417
   6200 Cynthia Drive
   Wilmer, Alabama 36587
   Loans (at present) of $500 to $100,000, at 8 to 25 percent, for up to ten years.

4. Universal
   Box 1100
   Montclair, New Jersey 07042

5. TranSouth
   2025 Mound Street
   Orange Park, Florida

6. Wellington Company
   449 Santa Fe Drive, Suite 900
   Encintas, California 92024

Note: Wellington's current full-page ad states that "free money is available for your business," but you should get all the details first.

7. Another possibility is a home equity loan:

   Sovran Equity Mortgage Corporation
   9485 Regency Square Boulevard
   Jacksonville, Florida 32225

   Note: It would be best to apply to a home equity company in your own city or region.

8. If you own life insurance policies, you may be able to obtain a loan based on the cash value of your policy.

9. Some people claim they have raised money by holding auctions. Unless you have a lot of valuable items, this probably won't work. Your success obviously depends on what you have to auction.

10. Some prosperous Arab companies have money to invest in companies. The following company offers a free report and states in its ad that "one transaction can make you independent for the rest of your life."

    International Middle East Association, Dept. DMM178
    419 North Newport Boulevard, Station B
    Newport Beach, California 92663

11. Small Business Association Loans (three kinds)

    1. SBA Guaranteed Loan—the most easily obtainable loan of this kind
       Contact: Director
               Office of Business Loans
               Small Business Administration
               1441 L Street, N.W., Washington, D.C. 20416

    2. The Immediate Participation Loan (limit of $350,000)
       This loan offers lower interest rates than a bank loan.
       Contact: Same address as SBA Guaranteed Loan

3. The Direct Loan—Hardest SBA loan to qualify for because the money is loaned directly.
   Contact: Associate Administrator for Management Assistance, same address as above.

NOTE: We cannot vouch for the quality and integrity of the companies listed above.

PART IV

Money-Making Techniques

Self-Publish Your Way to Success

The self-publishing concept is that just about anybody with a good book idea, mail-order operators included, can write it, publish it, and try to sell it. Mail-order operators have a real advantage here, because they can offer the book through their companies. Since they already know how to place ads and have an operation in place for filling orders, they have an edge on doing well with a book product.

All manner of mail-order books and booklets are being sold on a variety of subjects ranging from how to stop smoking to how to build a more successful career. Books on solar energy have done well. The publishers of such books run classified or display ads in leading mail-order publications, filling orders as they're received.

Every book is a "lead" book for a self-publisher. During the first year of a book's release, a self-publisher builds a solid market for a future of sustained sales. A major national publisher may sell only 5,000 copies of a book, total, but a self-publisher can often sell that many or a great deal more, year after year. Much depends on the book and how effective the advertising for it is.

There's no telling where a self-publishing venture may lead you in mail-order. While you must pay for the printing of the book and its advertising, you also keep all the profits. By comparison, most large publishers offer only a 10 to 15 percent royalty rate. But remember that a large publisher is also taking the risk and paying for the printing and distribution of the book.

Remember the success story of Joe Karbo, reported earlier in this book? He became a millionaire as a self-publisher. Do you think he would have done that well if he had worked with a traditional book publisher? The odds are heavily against it. But keep in mind that Karbo came up with a brilliant and captivating ad for his book. It was his four-star, magnetic advertising that brought in thousands and thousands of orders. And he got to keep all the profits.

Still, you should be aware of both sides of the coin. A book you self-publish may turn out to be a bomb. Some self-publishers report that even after extensive promotion and advertising, their books have sold very few copies. With more than 56,000 titles now being published each year in the United States alone, there's a lot of competition out there.

So there's no way to predict what might happen for you in a self-publishing venture. With your experience and knowledge of how to sell other items by mail, you might do very well with a self-published book. Just realize that it entails a risk. But isn't every new product or service item you launch a risk? Your first self-published book might bring you a small profit, do fairly well, or earn you a fortune. It might also bomb and not even recover its production and promotion costs. By the same token, your first venture could bomb, but then you could make a lot of money on your second try.

Bennett Cerf, publisher and founder of Random House, once said, "The book business is really a very stable industry. People keep on buying books, even in the midst of a national crisis." So at least that much is certain. The public is going to keep on buying books. Millions of them. How large a share of the pie you will realize will depend on a number of factors:

timing, advertising, demand for the book, its appeal, how well you coordinate ads, and so on.

If you decide to sell a self-published book via your mail-order company, you should be aware that many self-publishers call their products "books" in their advertisements. In reality, what they call books often turn out to be skimpy pamphlets, folios, or booklets. I believe this is deceptive because there's a definite difference between a book and a pamphlet. The word "book" implies a full-length work between covers. To raise such an issue, of course, takes us into the ethics of advertising.

What customers are buying is not the book, but the information it contains, so many buyers simply don't care if the "book" is only ten pages or so in actual length. Still, my own feelings on the question are that an advertiser should call the product a pamphlet if that's what it is rather than to imply that the buyer is going to receive a full-length book.

BUILD A LIST OF YOUR OWN CUSTOMERS

The most valuable mailing list you can have is the list of your own customers. If you offer good, sound, useful, and attractive products, your customers will buy from you time and again. And with each new customer name you add, your list becomes more valuable.

How do you build a customer list? If you've been in the mail-order business for some time, then you already know the answer to this question. You start compiling a customer list with your first sale. In a few months, you see your customer list growing consistently, if, that is, your ads are effective and bringing results.

If a customer is pleased with your product, he or she is likely to remember it, and the name of your company as well. When you send such customers another offer by direct mail or they see another of your ads pitching a different product item, they will be influenced to buy from you again. On the other hand, if they were not pleased with their first purchases, they may well take a pass on your current offer.

I strongly recommend that you keep a careful record of every person who sends you an order. (Notice I said *order* and not inquiry. An inquiry is a request for more details on whatever you're offering. An order is a genuine purchase of your product.) You should make it a priority to record the full name and address of every person who orders from you. Some mail-order operators record this information in three-ring notebooks with columns for name, address, city, state, product ordered, price paid, and method of payment. Other mail-order firms put the information on index cards or computers. It's up to you how you wish to record the names. Just do it. Don't lose one of the most important and valuable commodities you can have in this business—a growing, dynamic customer list.

If you have a secretary or assistant, that person can enter this information. See that it gets done without delay. I urge you to have the names of your customers typed, or at least hand-printed. If you have an assistant write out the names by hand, you may not be able to read the names correctly the next time you want to send your customers an offer. It's far better to type or print them neatly. And keep them in a special place: a desk- or file-drawer or a file-card box specifically dedicated to this purpose.

There's a special reward if you are careful with your customer list and compile the names neatly and accurately. Once you get enough of them, say five or ten thousand, you can offer them to list companies for substantial amounts of money. Your customer list can one day be a significant source of income for you. So keep up with them; your customer names are like money in the bank.

USE A-I-D-A: ATTENTION-INTEREST-DESIRE-ACTION

One of this book's strongest messages is that the more effective your ads are, the more orders you will receive and the more money you'll make. So your focus when working on ads should be on persuasion. You're not trying to be cute or to entertain the prospect. Spending money is serious business. If you're going to lead a prospect to send you an order, your ad has to convince him or her to take action. When asked if advertising was entertainment, veteran advertising executive David Ogilvy replied, "I do not regard advertising as entertainment."

One of the best investments you can make in your advertising future is to buy a copy of the famous book written by advertising genius Claude Hopkins. I've mentioned it before; it's called *Scientific Advertising*. Copywriters everywhere have been mining the gold in this masterful work for years, and your first reading will inspire you to return to it again and again. I first read it many years ago, and I continue, time and again, to refer to it.

Your job as an advertiser is to move the product. You're after a sale and not out to amuse, get a laugh, or entertain, even if these may sometimes be the by-products of a good advertisement.

There are four basis steps in a strong ad:

- Attention
- Interest
- Desire
- Action

Let's take a more detailed look at each step in the process of leading a prospect to read your entire ad and then send you an order immediately.

Attention

It can't be said too many times: If your ads don't grab people's attention, you're dead in the water. There are just too many competing ads for prospects to look at. In my view, the "attention" step is the most important of all. There's no chance of your making a sale if prospects quit reading your ad and turn the page or throw your sales letter away.

Consider this headline for elevator shoes:

Headline: Makes You Almost 2" Taller!

That grabs your attention. It hooked mine, even though I'm not in the market for elevator shoes. And here's another attention-getter:

>   *Headline:* The Very Finest in Golf!

Anyone interested in golf who sees that ad opener would almost be compelled to read more.

Now look at this one from the *Wall Street Journal*:

>   *Headline:* The rich didn't get that way by being idle.

Doesn't that opener make you want to find out what the ad is all about? It did for me.

Interest

Okay. Let's say you did a good job in grabbing attention. The second step is to create interest. This is often tough to do in a small classified ad where you don't have many words to work with. It's easier in a fairly large space ad or in a sales letter.

Ways to instill interest are often found in the product or service you're selling. When working on an ad, think about the item you're offering. What is its chief appeal? Jot down some notes about it. Does it appeal to both men and women? Will it protect the prospect, make money for him or her, help launch a business, improve fitness, make a vacation more enjoyable, or what? In the product's main attractions you can usually find ideas for creating interest in it. Here are a few examples:

- Women—How to Land an Executive Job!
- Fastest, Easiest Piano Course in History!
- Mail-order Millionaire Helps Beginners Make $750 Weekly!
- New Luxury Car Without Cost!
- Borrow Up to $25,000 Without Interest!

These are good openers for ads meant to bring in inquiries. They would interest potential buyers in asking for more details. If your goal is to sell directly from the ad, it will take more words to create interest.

Desire

I believe one of the best ways to instill desire for the items you're offering is to use a combination of words and phrases in your ads that enable prospects to see themselves using your product or enjoying a better, richer lifestyle because they bought your product or service. Here's an example:

Headline: Bank increasing profits monthly!

This message creates a picture. The prospect can see himself or herself inside a bank making a large deposit. In other words, the flame of desire must be fanned to get prospects to move to the next step of taking action. This is obviously easier to do if you use a sales letter with two or four pages. If you're trying to do it in a display or classified ad, you're clearly more limited.

Film immortal Edward G. Robinson fanned the flame of his true desire. He of course enjoyed his successful acting career, but his real desire was to collect beautiful paintings. Even when he was a boy, his desire was already tugging at him. "Long before long pants," he said, "I haunted New York's museums and art galleries. How I longed in those days to take home some of the paintings that gave me so much pleasure."

As Robinson's film career grew and he prospered, pictures began to cover the walls of his Beverly Hills home. His example shows what can happen when you fan the flame of your desire. Beginning with a picture he bought for $2.00 in 1913, Robinson built one of the finest private collections in the United States, valued in the millions.

Fan the flame of your own desire both in your efforts to run magnetic ads and in building a growing, increasingly successful mail-order company.

Action

In trying to motivate potential buyers to take action, you're fighting the prospect's natural procrastination. A number of techniques can be used to communicate to prospects that they should not delay but should take action today, and preferably right away. The following are psychological strategies that have worked for many mail-order companies:

- Communicate the idea that the prospect will be left behind unless he or she orders.
- Use the idea that the prospect is not getting any younger.
- State that stock of your product could run out at any time, or that you're not sure how much longer you can offer the item.
- Let prospects know that your asking price will soon be going up, but that if their orders are received by a certain deadline they'll be sure to receive the product at the current price. Time limits do much to propel prospects to take action and buy.
- Simply state flat out that the prospect will regret it if he or she does not get your product. Some advertisers go a step further and say that prospects will probably never get another chance to own such a unique and useful product.
- If your product involves the customer's joining something, or ''being an applicant,'' you can use the idea that your company is not sure how much longer applicants will be accepted.
- Imply or state explicitly that the prospect's income will start increasing once the product, plan, or program is in his or her hands. In other words, let prospects know that money could be lost if they don't order soon.
- Say that extra money ''could have been in your pocket today'' if the prospect had ordered earlier. (This assumes the product is some kind of money-making plan.)
- Use the postdated check option, saying that the prospect's check won't be cashed for 30 days after he or she has received the product. This delays your getting your money, but it can bring in many additional orders.

- Communicate the idea that, by ordering, the prospect will be following in your successful footsteps.
- Use a sentence like, "If I don't keep my promise to you [regarding what the product will do], you'll never order from me again." This says to prospects that the promise will be fulfilled.
- Stress that the prospect won't get cheated by ordering your plan, item, or program.
- Use the idea that the prospect "deserves" to have the product in his or her life.

COPING WITH SKEPTICISM

One problem that most members of the mail-order industry continually face is that of customer skepticism. Skepticism is a thief because it can rob you of many sales. The best place to try to deal with it is in your sales letters, where you have more space than in a classified or display ad.

What causes skepticism? Perhaps the major cause is that some of the prospects who see your ads and read your sales letters have had bad experiences with other mail-order firms. An ad or letter may have misrepresented a product or service; a firm may never have filled an order or not followed through on something originally promised. Here are some reliable, proven ways to combat a prospect's skepticism:

1. Try to make every word count whether you're using an ad or a sales letter.
2. Emphasize that your company is highly reputable and that your selling practices are ethical. Remind your prospect of your guarantee, the other satisfied buyers you've had, the length of time you've been in business, and your commitment to fill all orders promptly.
3. If you have or can obtain honest testimonials praising your product or service, use them. (You only have room to do this in large space ads and direct-mail sales letters.)
4. Write a creed, or personal philosophy, of advertising. State this creed at the top of your full-page ads and sales

ADVERTISING IS LIKE A GAME OF CHESS

In his fascinating book, *Scientific Advertising*, Claude Hopkins states that "advertising is much like a game of chess." In a real sense, the profession of selling, whether in print, via commercials, or face-to-face, is indeed like making moves on a chessboard. A headline opens this kind of chess game and hooks the reader into reading more of the ad.

In chess, players try to get their opponents to move their pieces in certain ways, thus setting up patterns that will lead to checkmate.

Of course a good ad doesn't trap the customer, but rather leads the prospect to a decision to buy. The steps of an effective ad are meant to lead the prospect to certain conclusions: that he or she needs the product or service, that the product will work or help, and that the prospect should buy now.

Hopkins emphasized the importance of his belief that the smart copywriter does not attack a rival. Rather, the copywriter's objective is to communicate the better features of the product or service, its appeal, usefulness, and overall attractiveness. These are the qualities that make prospects reach for their checkbooks and credit cards.

"The only purpose of advertising is to make sales."
Claude Hopkins

"Don't try to be amusing. Money spending is a serious matter. The more you tell the more you sell."
Claude Hopkins

---

letters. It need not be a long statement. Here's an example: "Dedicated to integrity and the highest possible standards of mail-order selling."

Even with such a creed, you still won't be able to land the most skeptical prospects. No matter how much selling skill, persuasive advertising copy, sincerity, and overall professionalism you run your business with, there will always be some prospects who won't yield. So after you've done everything in your power to overcome their doubts but without success, you had better cross them off the list and forget them. Life is too short. There are too many others out there who will buy from you.

Keep this in mind whenever you fail to sell to an overly skeptical person: For every prospect you are unable to land, there are a hundred others you can sell to. Forget the impossible ones and move on to those you can lead to buying action. Hang in there when you receive little notes from prospects saying they don't believe your ads or doubt your products will do what you say. Just think to yourself: "Here comes some more modern-day skepticism, but I can and will handle it. I'll do my utmost to save this sale." Being the confident professional you are, you're sure to save a lot of them.

FULL-PAGE VERSUS SMALLER ADS

The cost, at this writing, of a full-page ad in one of the well-known mail-order publications is $3,733.80. This figure will no doubt rise. Other publications often used in the business charge even higher amounts.

Full-page ads, however, are a powerful way to advertise. By combining a magazine's circulation with the number of "pass-along" nonsubscribers who also read it, you can see how a full-page ad can potentially reach millions. If your ad persuades prospects to send in their orders, you can make a lot of money.

Joe Karbo became a millionaire using full-page ads. But remember one important fact. Karbo knew he had a winning ad when he ran it. He tested each ad a number of times before running it as a full-pager. And he improved and perfected his ads over a period of time so that when they appeared, he was confident they would be successful. Reportedly, he was surprised at just how powerful some of his ads were.

The point is clear. Unless and until you're sure you have a four-star, powerful full-page ad, as well as the money to risk by running it, stick to smaller ads. Test and test again. Make it your business to find out where your ad is weak. Then rewrite it, polish it, and perfect it. If your tests prove successful, make your decision to run a full-pager. Better still, you could condense your ad and run it as a third- or half-page ad. A popular

LETTERHEAD INSERTION ORDER

Here is a sample advertising insertion order, very similar to the forms issued by leading mail-order publications. Feel free to adapt it for your own use. Include the 15 percent discount line if you are using your ad-agency letterhead.

MIDWEST ADVERTISING COMPANY
17639 Windcrest Street
Des Moines, Iowa 25000
(515) 000–0000

Product advertised: (State the nature of product-booklet, service, etc.)

Heading: (Business Opportunities, Do-It-Yourself, or other category)

Publication in which ad is to appear: (name of publication)

Date ad is to appear: (date or month of issue in which ad will appear)

Number of times ad is to be run: (one or more times)

Key: (Type in your code for the ad.)

Number of words in ad: (total number of words)

Copy for ad: (Leave enough space so that all the words of your ad can

be included.)

Rate Per Word: <u>(Insert the rate per word charged by the publication.)</u>

Subtotal: _____

Minus 15 percent agency discount: _____

Total amount enclosed for this ad: _____

mail-order publication currently charges $1,859.20 for a one-third-page ad.

A one-sixth-page ad costs even less. The mail-order publication mentioned above charges $945.70 for a one-sixth-page ad. That's about half the cost of a one-third-page ad. The smaller ads will give you an indication of your copy's pulling power. You can start with a one-sixth-page ad and then move up gradually, a step at a time, till you're at the full-page level.

HOW TO SAVE MONEY ON ALL YOUR ADS

Experienced mail-order operators are aware of the value of having their own in-house ad agencies. Give your own agency a name and have separate letterhead printed just for it. Then, whenever you run ads, whatever the size, send in your insertion orders on agency letterhead. Most leading mail-order publications know what you're doing, but they don't mind. They want your advertising dollars and will allow you the standard 15 percent agency discount on gross billings. The savings can be considerable when you're running large and small display ads and classifieds in a number of publications. In fact, when you use the pyramiding-your-profits strategy discussed earlier, this 15 percent discount will save you a bundle.

Use the sample letterhead ad-insertion form included in this chapter to design one for your own agency. Most mail-order publications will send you their own ad-insertion form when you request one. You can adapt those forms, too, by putting your agency's name at the top and having the copies you need run off. Then, each time you wish to run an ad in a particular publication, fill in your adapted version of its form and mail it in with your payment, minus the 15 percent standard discount.

To get the rates on the various ad sizes from mail-order publications, just write to them on your company or ad-agency letterhead and request their rate cards and advertising kits. Many will send you elaborate kits with all the information you need about running ads in their publications. You also need the information in their kits to learn the deadlines for getting ad copy in, to make sure your ads appear in the issues you want them to.

Unless you're an experienced mail-order veteran, I urge you not to even think about larger size page ads until you've gained enough skill and confidence in running both classified and very small display ads. Meanwhile, watch for effective larger page ads and save the ones you think are strong. Ask yourself if the ad would persuade you to send in an order, if you were a prospect reading it for the first time. Break down the elements of success of these larger ads. Are different sections and headings used? Why? What kind of guarantees are used? Any bonus extras? In other words, study them and file the ones you want to save for future reference.

One day, after your company has grown and expanded, newcomers to the industry may well be referring to *your* full-page ads for sales-technique ideas. At that happy point, you'll be in the mail-order big time. Never forget that full-page ads have the power to bring you an avalanche of orders.

Set Your Priorities and Stick to Them

The shortest route to success in the mail-order industry is to determine what your priorities are and then to stick to them. If you've been operating a mail-order company for any length of time, you're already aware of the importance of knowing what your priorities are and following through on them every day.

By priorities, I simply mean your need to focus constantly on the most important aspects of running your company. To help you set your own, here is a worthy list of priorities I set for my own company some time ago. Many mail-order firms have a similar focus. You may wish to add other areas of your own selection to this basic list:

1. Your lead product or service
2. Type or kinds of advertising
3. Choice of mail-order publications to use
4. Copy preparation (strong copy for your ads)
5. Testing

6. Your advertising objective and strategy
7. Filling orders
8. Direct mail (when you're ready to use it)
9. Keeping records
10. Finding good, reliable printing companies
11. Studying successful ads and direct-mail sales letters
12. Researching new product and service ideas

Notice how the list covers almost all phases of operating a mail-order company. Your own list of priorities might be longer or shorter than this. That's OK. But whatever length or ranking order you use, I urge you to write down your own set of priorities. It will help you to see at a glance the various aspects of running your company.

Look over your own set of priorities and place a star or check mark beside those areas you believe are most important. In reality, every single aspect is crucial to your success. But if all of them are so vital, how can you find the time to give each area? All you can do is your best. Obviously, some of the aspects will not get enough of your time and attention during busy periods. When that happens, and it will, you'll simply have to decide which areas need your immediate attention, and which can wait.

If your lead offer bombs, then you clearly need to give prompt attention to coming up with another feature product or service. What I'm saying is this. If what you hoped would be your number-one product does poorly, you go back to the drawing-board (with research files in hand) to come up with a new offer that will click. Put your focus where it's needed most.

If your company grows and prospers and you're able to hire assistants to help run your business, then you can put employees in charge of some of these priority areas. Copy preparation, however, is so important that you should probably always handle this phase of your business yourself. But assistants could be of help in finding and dealing with printers, selecting publications for your ads, recordkeeping, investigating mailing lists, and doing research on possible new products and offers.

When your offers start pulling hundreds, or thousands, of orders, you'll definitely need help to open all your mail, handle the money, and fill the orders promptly. You can wait until that point before thinking about hiring part-time assistants. If you live near a college campus, you'll probably have no trouble hiring some reliable students to help open mail and fill orders. But they should be screened and interviewed carefully so you can be sure they are dependable, will show up to do the work, and will get it done correctly and efficiently.

BUY LOW AND SELL HIGH

"The way to make money—lots of it—in mail-order is to be able to produce your product for a small cost and then sell it by mail for a considerably larger price." I heard and read this many times after entering mail-order. It's become a general operating principle of the business. Don't misinterpret it, though. It does *not* mean you should cheat the customer. It means you should pick a product that is inexpensive for you to buy or manufacture. Then mark up the price high enough to give you a good profit when you sell it by mail.

A point made often in this book is that many of the large space ads you see these days use the words "plan," "book," "program," and "system" to describe the items they offer. In reality, most of these turn out to be ten- or 20-page pamphlets, booklets, or folios. It takes no genius to realize that it only costs the advertisers of these items pennies to have copies printed. A 15-page pamphlet, for example, may cost only 80¢ per copy, if a large print-run is ordered. If the mail-order operator turns around and sells each copy for $15.00 or $20.00 (which many of them are doing), then he or she is making a profit of more than 15 or 20 times what it cost to produce the item.

Still, I personally believe strongly in giving customers good value for their hard-earned dollars. While it's true that many buyers are paying for the information in these booklets and simply don't care how brief and flimsy they are, I believe many who send in orders end up feeling misled by the ads they answered.

To build a mail-order company that will last and grow more prosperous over the years ahead, I urge you to give your customers good value for their money. Sure, it's OK to sell a small booklet or manual; just make sure that the information it contains is really helpful to buyers. Then they won't mind the few pages. If there's little of value in what you sell, some of your buyers will let you know about it. Worse, they won't buy from you again. And many may ask for refunds.

THE RIGHT COMBINATION FOR YOUR CATALOG

American Express just sent me a new mail-order catalog called "A Collection of Select Products from Around the World." How's that for a catalog title? Not bad.

The front cover of the catalog shows a young couple out on the town in formal evening clothes. In the lower lefthand section of the cover, six special features of the catalog are listed to catch your eye and interest:

- No finance charges
- Satisfaction guaranteed
- Assured shopping
- Performance-tested products
- Products selected for value
- 24-hour toll-free phone services

American Express gave its catalog a theme: autumn in New York. The cover photo fits this theme beautifully. In my opinion, it's really a clever, sophisticated catalog.

A second catalog, in the same mail, was sent from the well-known catalog company, Hanover House. It has 96 pages of items, all shown in full color, which the American Express catalog also used. Since both were fall-season catalogs, each featured Christmas products and tree-trimming accessories. But each catalog contained a wide variety of other items, including the following:

Car drinking-mug
Car window deicer
Wicker-weave bookcase
Porcelain knobs
Family message center
Glass religious plaque

Long-lasting light bulbs
"Singing" flowers
Therapeutic neck pillow
Breakfast tray
Sheet straps (that hold bed sheets in place)
Gown with a built-in bra
Cameras
Stereos
Cordless radar detectors
Laptop word processors
Cellular phones
Home safe
Angel candle holder
Complete foreign language courses (Spanish, French, Italian, German, Japanese, Chinese, Hebrew, Arabic)
Sewing kit
Indoor/outdoor thermometer
Pencil sharpener
Mini lint brush
"Super clip" containers (to keep food sealed and fresh)
Colorful nail clippers
Rainbow paper clips
Deviled-egg plate
"Amazing Answers" board (over 130 questions and answers)
Seven-piece cake-decorating set
Money magnets
Soap crayons
Easy-to-read playing cards (printed in extra large type)
Stay-put rain chapeau (covers hairdos without crushing them)
Anti-fog cloth
Jogging suit
Brass seagull plaque
Set of 50 pairs of earrings
Car lunch box
Surprise boxes
Four-room wood dollhouse
Curio cabinet
Nylon satin slippers

Three-piece gem set
Recliner slipcover
Filter pitcher (purifies water)
Musical pencil case
Arctic explorers' gloves
Snow pusher
Eyeglass holder
Marriage plaque
"Massage" sandals

When you're ready to produce your own mail-order catalog, you'll need to decide on the right combination of products. The success formula for many effective catalogs is a combination of basic, staple items that are proven sellers and hard-to-find products. Car lunch boxes, for example, are not difficult to find. But "singing" flowers and "massage" sandals would be relatively hard to find in stores. Using the catalog items listed above, as examples, the idea is to go for a mix of regulars (like nail clippers, food containers, lint brushes, eyeglass holders) and rather unusual items (like bed-sheet straps, soap crayons, and the "Amazing Answers" board).

The pitfall many mail-order firms fall into is trying to grow too swiftly with catalog sales. When this happens, the quality of service can drop and customers become dissatisfied. The L. L. Bean Company, which offers clothing and products for the outdoors, is a famous mail-order firm that prides itself on the high-quality service it has provided to customers for many years. But, at this writing, L. L. Bean has concluded that it has been growing too quickly. Bean's promise over the years has been "100 percent satisfaction or your money back," but in 1988 a lot of customers were not satisfied and, according to the *Wall Street Journal*, "returned $82 million worth of goods . . . or about 14 percent of the company's $588 million in sales." These returns cost Bean $18 million in shipping and handling costs and lost the firm a National Quality Award (for service) from the Department of Commerce.

To counter this drop in customer satisfaction, the Bean Company hired a Harvard Business School consultant and announced a new service theme to its 3,500 employees in a special meeting. The new theme is strong: "Get it right the first time."

The Bean Company's original expansion target was a whopping billion dollars in sales by 1992. This objective has now been shelved. In the words of Bean's president, "We would like to grow at a rate of about five percent to eight percent over the next few years," compared with a growth rate of 23 percent a year over the last decade.

L. L. Bean plans to spend several million dollars over the next few years to improve service. This money will be spent in the following ways:

1. Revising catalogs
2. Retraining employees to make sure they can find out what customers really want
3. Conducting a survey of present customers
4. Upgrading computers so the company can offer more detailed descriptions of its merchandise

A common reason for returning merchandise is because clothes and shoes don't fit. But buyers of many different kinds of products are changing, and according to Stanley Fenvessy, a New York mail-order consultant, they "are becoming more demanding." Fenvessy says, "They know they can be more demanding, given the competition between mail-order merchants and retailers."

So if and when you launch your own company's catalog, you should strive for a high degree of service and satisfaction. Catalog customers are money in the bank—the catalog business now amounts to $35 billion each year. They'll keep buying from you for years to come if they're treated right and given first-class service. In fact, through the 1990s and beyond, you can beat your catalog competition by focusing on these two areas. The companies that deliver in the areas of service and satisfaction will be the ones that get the most business.

TELL-ALL COPY VERSUS VAGUE GENERALITIES

Claude Hopkins frequently said that "the more you tell the more you sell," but a case is frequently made for not telling everything, for teasing the prospect a bit and making him or her

MAIL-ORDER IS FOR WOMEN, TOO

More women are gaining success as entrepreneurs today, but why has this development been so long in coming? There are many reasons, of course, but two major ones are that many women have either accepted their traditionally limited roles or have not been able to see ways to break out of and go beyond those roles.

Jo Foxworth, head of her own advertising agency and author of *Boss Lady* (Warner), believes that cultural barriers have prevented women from moving into top business positions. "We haven't set our sights high enough. We haven't tried to break patterns of the past. One way women have held themselves back is by hiding behind their petticoats when they make mistakes. Men admit error so easily, but we take it so personally and brood about it, when it may not have been our fault to begin with."

But women are becoming wiser in the ways of business every day. More women are reaching out for something more—meaning a greater sense of accomplishment, higher pay, bigger challenges, achievement in business, and all kinds of increased fulfillment in their life and work. A prosperous career in mail-order is one of the many ways a woman today can achieve that satisfaction.

---

want to know more about the product. If everything is told, so this argument goes, the prospect may not order since nothing remains to be revealed and his or her curiosity hasn't been stimulated. Perhaps the best course of action is to find a happy medium between telling too much and telling too little. Many, however, still basically agree with the Hopkins view. If you must choose between the two ways, you should probably tell more than you withhold. You're of course limited by the number of words in small classified ads, and that's one reason classified are often used just to produce a flow of inquiries.

With display ads, you have additional room to tell more about the product or service. Direct-mail sales letters, which can run up to eight pages, offer the most room for telling a lot. I've seen eight-page sales letters that have told just about everything that could be told. They have held my attention and interest until the end of the last page.

Depending upon your offer, you can test to see if telling a lot about the product works better or not as well as telling a little. This latter method is known as "teaser copy." The idea is to tell potential buyers what the item is *not*, without revealing what it actually is. Many advertisers are very creative in coming up with effective teaser copy. Consider the following display ad for the *Country Curtains* catalog:

Headline: Free Color Catalog
Body copy: Over 100 styles of curtains trimmed with ruffles, fringe and lace . . . tab, tailored and ruffled styles in warm colors and floral prints, some insulated, balloon curtains, lots of lace, bed ensembles and many home decorating accessories.

The ad closed with the company's name and address. It certainly gave a lot of information about products, but as you may have noticed, no prices were stated. The clear description of the curtains no doubt resulted in a large number of inquiries. Then the company would have answered each inquiry with more details, pictures of the curtains, and prices.

The ad's purpose was to produce inquiries. But even so, a lot of facts were given. The nature of the product was made clear. The variety of styles, colors, and fabrics available was communicated in the ad. Your ad copy should be polished and perfected until there are no vague generalities left—only crisp, clear, compelling phrases that bring the item to life in the mind's eye of your potential customers.

THE CASE FOR A YEARLY SALES GOAL

What does a sales goal do for your mail-order company? First, it gives you a definite track to run on, an objective to shoot for. Second, a goal helps you achieve your desired results. You need a goal in order to measure how you are doing. You can set a sales goal for each month and an overall goal for the entire year.

The Importance of an Early Goal

Don't make the mistake of waiting too long to set a goal for your mail-order sales. The earlier you have a goal to focus on the better.

When comedian Bob Hope was a young, struggling comic in Ohio many years back, he felt lucky to get $5.00 for an evening's work. He had to appear in some tough places in order to keep working. But Hope hung in there. He set his goal: to rise to better bookings in nicer clubs for more money. He stuck to his goal and began his climb to remarkable success on the national scene. A part in a Broadway play turned out to be his big break, and today he is an international star.

The Power of Thinking About Your Sales Goal

Psychologists have said for years that continually thinking about a major goal or objective over a period of time builds up a certain degree of power behind that goal and helps a person achieve it. So after you set a certain mail-order sales goal, try to begin seeing yourself actually getting there. Visualize yourself in the process of beating your earlier sales goals. Assume that you can and will reach your goal, and expect the sales of your dreams to come true.

Make no mistake about this method. There is definite power in it. It is faith in action—the very method that has put people from all walks of life at the top of the success ladder. What helps you to achieve the goal you set is the challenge behind it. It's the challenge that stimulates you and influences you to accomplish more than you may once have thought you could.

Commitment Plus Action Equals Success

Most of the top people in mail-order, and in sales in general, no matter what the product or service they sell may be, are dedicated to their jobs. They live, breathe, and sleep their work. They are very serious about the goals they set from year to year, and they do their utmost to realize them.

Goal Setting Is a Must

Frank Bettger, one of the great salesmen of the century, raised his sales production level like magic when he began to set goals and back up those goals with direct action.

As a teenager, Benjamin Franklin, one of the founding fathers of the United States, showed that he thought goals were important. He read widely and set himself the goal of learning the art of writing. He planned his work and then worked his plan, which is also a sound method for running your mail-order company. Late in life, Franklin said that he had been able to accomplish all he did because of his writing ability.

A Plan for Setting and Achieving Your Mail-Order Goals

Here are some proven steps for reaching your goals in mail-order:

1. Decide what you will have to do to reach your sales goals for each year.
2. Have both short-range and long-range goals. When you achieve an easier goal, the confidence you'll receive will help lead you to the attainment of more difficult goals.
3. Set realistic goals. Determine what you want to achieve in the mail-order business over a period of years.
4. Plan the key steps needed to reach each of your goals.
5. Resolve to accomplish what you've set for yourself, and express your decision each and every day. Stay committed to your goals.
6. Put plenty of action behind the sales goal you set.
7. Be ready to adapt. You may have to change certain steps in your plan, or even to work out an entirely new plan of action to reach your goal.
8. Once you attain a goal, set a new one and start the process over again. Always have a goal in front of you to keep yourself moving forward.

Set a *realistic* goal for each year. A realistic goal takes all possible factors into account. If you set an unrealistic goal, you may get discouraged before the year is even half over. So do some serious thinking about your overall goal in advance of deciding for certain on it, and make sure that the goal is one it's possible to achieve.

Don't Set Your Mail-Order Sales Goal Too Low

On the other hand, don't settle for too low a sales goal. You want to be a mail-order pro who is continually advancing, so make sure you establish an ever-rising sales objective for each new year or six-month period. There may be times during the year when the goal you have determined looks hard to reach. Don't get discouraged at these low points. Know that you have the power within you to achieve your goal and that even at such times you are moving steadily closer to the success you desire with the new orders you receive and the sales you make each day.

Don't Give Up on Your Goal

"Hold on with a bulldog grip, and chew and choke as much as possible," wrote Lincoln in his telegram to Grant. A quicker way of saying the same thing is "stick to your goal." There is real power in the idea of not giving up. Where would the United States be if the founding fathers had given up in 1776? What would the fate of the Union have been if Abe Lincoln had given up his determination to preserve it?

One day in the late 1940s, while at the controls of a test plane, Howard Hughes suddenly found himself in real trouble. Rather than bail out and lose the most expensive plane he owned, he crash-landed it. He lived through it, though he was badly scarred and burned. But Hughes really won that test. He refused to give up in the face of death itself.

THREE USEFUL TOOLS FOR YOUR MAIL-ORDER ACHIEVEMENT

You can realize your sales goal for every year if you chart your course carefully and don't take any detours. Three vital tools will help you to attain the mail-order success you want. Guard them well. They are

- Your judgment
- Your ability to work smarter, harder, and more effectively
- Your good health

All three are needed to go far in the mail-order business. If you feel you are weak in any of the three areas, work on improving it. You can develop your judgment, industry, and your ability to work smarter and harder. Above all, see that you maintain good health.

Your judgment is essential to your success in mail-order selling, so strive always to absorb knowledge and the power to use it. Whatever you do, continue advancing toward your mail-order sales goals. A real champion, a star in the business, never loses sight of his or her objectives.

Maintaining a Competitive Edge

One of the best ways to beat a lot of your mail-order competition is by filling orders quickly and accurately. From my own experience, I know that buyers are pleased and impressed when the mail-order company they order from sends them their orders promptly.

Some mail-order firms run ads for a product even before they have it in stock. They are then forced to delay filling orders until they can get the item printed or manufactured. And that takes time.

To build goodwill and a reputation for professionalism in this business, you must treat all orders with top priority. A brief delay in filling orders is sometimes unavoidable. Some periods will be busier for you than others. Holidays and weekends cause delays. Most customers who buy from you won't mind a short delay. Just do your best to get each and every order filled as promptly as possible. Your reward will be a growing number of satisfied customers, assuming, of course, that they like the items they buy from you.

When customers mail orders to your company, they start to look forward to receiving the items. If you take too long to get the items to them, then you're going to have some unhappy customers, and a number of them may never order from your company again. I remember mail-order firms to which I sent orders that took a month, six weeks, or longer to fill. In fact, some never sent my orders, even after I sent a written complaint or phoned to tell them I never got the order. Do you think I ordered from these companies again?

Be aware that federal law now states that mail-order companies must fill orders within 30 days, or send a refund. This doesn't mean that a mail-order firm can wait 30 days before responding to an order. It means that the order must be received by the customer *within* 30 days. Some mail-order companies violate this law. If you take more than 30 days to get orders to your customers, you run the risk of having complaints about your company made to the postal authorities.

It's also like pouring gasoline on a fire to ask for several extra dollars in your ads or sales letters for postage and handling costs and then to take four weeks, two months, or longer, to get the orders out. Some customers may report your company to postal authorities or to the magazines and mail-order publications in which your ads appear. So first-class customer service should be a hallmark of your company's credo. Run your company on the foundation of the Golden Rule, treating all customers as you would wish to be treated, and there's no telling how far you can go in the business.

WILD AND EXTRAVAGANT CLAIMS AROUSE SUSPICION

The Quaker Oats Company, at this writing, is being sued by the state of Texas on the charge that the company's ads for oat bran and oatmeal falsely claimed that eating the cereal lowered cholesterol and hence the risk of heart attack. A number of food companies have recently been hit with such lawsuits. In the words of the Texas attorney general, ''We're in the middle of an oat-bran craze in this country that was started by Quaker in order to sell its products. Consumers have been duped.''

As reported earlier in this book, a great number of display ads offer the opportunity to make huge amounts of money and achieve ''financial independence''—if prospects will just send in their orders. Take it from me, the large majority of these quick routes to riches are impractical, unworkable schemes. I've ordered and checked out quite a few. In many cases, the ads were either misleading or built around claims that were simply too extravagant.

While it's true that the great promoter and showman P. T. Barnum did say ''There's a sucker born every minute,'' his philosophy and practice was to try always to give customers honest entertainment value for their money. If your ads are sheer pie-in-the-sky, you may get a lot of orders at first, but you'll also get many requests for refunds. Complaints may be sent to the publications in which your ads appear. You will miss a lot of orders from those potential buyers who just refuse to believe wild claims of reaping incredible wealth in just 60 or 90 days.

Never forget that today's mail-order customers are becoming more demanding. Many are smarter than they used to be about what they order and from which companies. More of them ask for refunds when dissatisfied or disappointed with purchases.

It's OK and very necessary to make your offers sound enticing and useful. But if your ads and sales letters go too far and try to make customers think they will be appearing on ''Lifestyles of the Rich and Famous'' within 60 or 90 days after ordering your company's product, then you've engaged in deceptive and misleading advertising. Extravagant claims can damage your company's reputation. Sooner or later such claims will short-circuit your company's future in the industry.

Build your mail-order future on the bedrock of truth in advertising, and you will do well. It's entirely possible to praise the key features of your products, without arousing the skepticism of your prospects. Stick with credibility and believability, giving honest value in your products and offers, and mail-order customers will flock to you.

THE COMPETITIVE EDGE

"**O**ur competitive edge? Number one, we know the business, and we are committed to it. Our family has been in the food business for 58 years; we have been in the lodging business for 30 years. It is the only business we know. We don't claim to be in the gambling business or even the real estate business as such. However, we have developed some expertise in designing and building hotels at a reasonable cost."

J. Willard Marriott, Jr.
Chairman of the Board
and President
Marriott Corporation

MONEY-BACK GUARANTEES
CREATE BUYER CONFIDENCE

One successful California mail-order firm has prided itself for many years on its unlimited money-back guarantee. The firm's ads state there is no time limit on refunding a dissatisfied buyer's money. The company has reportedly given refunds as many as several years after an order was originally filled. Needless to say, this mail-order firm's refund requests are few and far between. They don't get many at all. On the contrary, many customers who have ordered from this company have taken the effort to write in to say how good they think the firm's products are. Now that's strong proof of customer satisfaction.

Many mail-order firms only offer limited 10-, 14-, or 30-day time limits on requesting your money back. So here's another way you can beat your competition. Offer unlimited money-back guarantees on your products. If you're uncomfortable with an unlimited guarantee, then offer a one-year time limit. If a customer hasn't returned an item and asked for a refund within a year, it's highly unlikely he or she will do so.

Even shorter guarantees are better than no guarantee at all. Use guarantees on all your offers. Use unlimited guarantees if at all possible. A confident customer is very often a repeat customer, and instilling buyer confidence is one of the most vital goals of a mail-order firm that intends to be around for a long time.

AVOID UNWORKABLE SCHEMES

Think how many more orders you can get by offering plans, programs, systems, ideas, and materials that really do what your ads and sales literature claim they do. That is the way to a fortune in mail-order.

One of the basic responsibilities of an honest, reliable mail-order company is to honor all requests for refunds, if, that is, ads run by the company guaranteed such refunds. Some ads, it's true, don't offer a money-back guarantee. The choice is yours whether or not to guarantee your product, but few mail-order firms become successful without honoring all refund requests on guaranteed products and offers. Word will spread fast if you refuse to send refunds to customers who are unhappy with what they received.

I know of mail-order companies that were doing well but then, once they stopped offering guarantees and quit honoring refund requests, didn't stay in business very long.

You don't want your company to fall by the wayside, especially after all the sacrifices you've made to build an established company. Here are some strong reasons for guaranteeing the products and items you offer:

- It's good business.
- It stimulates confidence in customers.
- It shows your company stands behind its products.
- It fosters good-will between your company and your customers.
- Money-back guarantees underscore the credibility of your advertising statements. When customers see your ads in the future, many will remember that you honored their

earlier refund requests and will feel safe in ordering again from you.

To sum up this chapter, you can maintain a strong competitive edge in the business by actively and continually applying the following guidelines:

1. Offer first-class customer service by filling each order promptly. Don't keep even one customer waiting.
2. Run your company on the foundation of the Golden Rule, offering genuine value for your customers' money.
3. Avoid any temptation to make wild, extravagant claims. Be persuasive and stress the good features of your products, but don't make hard-to-believe claims unless you can back them up. Stick with believability.
4. Definitely offer money-back guarantees on all your items. The unlimited-time guarantee, especially, can do a lot to build customer confidence.
5. Avoid offering far-fetched, unworkable, impractical schemes.
6. Keep a file of persuasive, compelling ads and sales letters. Study them frequently and strive to improve the appeal and power of your own ads and sales literature.
7. Keep up with what other mail-order companies are selling and their prices, ads, and sales letters. Occasionally order some of your competitors' items and compare them with your own.

Practical Considerations

Just as stock market investors need to be careful not to become too attached to certain stocks, you should be careful about putting too much stake in a brand-new, untested product or service. It might of course be a brilliant idea. But it could also backfire, end up not selling, and drain your company's profits away.

What sometimes appears to be a great new avenue may turn out to be a detour that could sidetrack you on the way to mail-order success. Blazing a new trail is risky, so proceed with caution.

A REPUTATION FOR QUALITY

According to the Small Business Administration, 63 percent of new businesses fail within six years. This high rate of new-business failures creates fear in the minds of those trying to launch their companies. Anything that can help your company to build a solid reputation for quality is worth your time and attention.

Japan's Reputation for Quality

In recent years, Japan has exploded on the international scene, taking a vital role on the world economic stage. Some Japanese refer to their country's spotlight importance as evidence that the ''Age of Japan'' is upon us.

A major reason for Japan's big success is the nation's dedication to quality products and performance. America's love for the Japanese-made Honda automobile is just one example of how the Japanese concern for quality wins consumer loyalty. American auto companies are fighting back, trying to produce better-quality cars, but in the view of many, Japan is still way out in front.

What is behind this Japanese success story? The standards followed by the Japanese didn't just spring up overnight and automatically. Consider the following influential factors:

1. Sheer hard work did much to improve Japan's productivity and the competitiveness of its products.
2. Japan has shown a remarkable ability to learn how to use foreign technology.
3. The Japanese demonstrate an increasing ability to conduct original research and to come up with innovations.

The originality of the Japanese is rapidly expanding and gives every indication of continuing to grow. A whopping 40 percent of the 1.2 million patents taken out worldwide in a recent year (the latest year for which there are records) were Japanese. Japan may well qualify as the entrepreneurial country of the twentieth century, or certainly of the century's last two decades.

There is no doubt that a reputation for quality can have a great impact on a nation's economic success. The same is true of your company's success in the mail-order industry. Establish a reputation as a company with high-quality standards, and your profits could well reach a very high level.

Guidelines for Getting a Reputation for Quality

How can you develop a reputation for quality? Here are some key ways:

- Offer quality products and services.
- Fill all orders promptly and professionally.
- Offer first-class service and stand behind the mail-order items you sell.
- Honor all refund requests promptly.
- Show your desire to offer genuine value to customers for their money.
- Use professional direct-mail sales letters.
- Foster a philosophy of truth in advertising, while still advertising effectively and persuasively.

CHECK OUT LISTS OF BUYER NAMES CAREFULLY

Once you make the decision to move into direct mail, or to test its effectiveness in selling some of your products and offers, you're really in the mail-order business in a big way. Name lists are available to you by the thousands. They cover every possible market, and each basic list can be broken down into specialized segments.

Let's take one market as an example. How about the baby-boomers? At present, one out of three people in the United States is a baby-boomer. That adds up to 75 million, which is a gigantic market. Baby-boomers were born between 1946 and 1964. As they mature, they show a growing demand for products and services that offer extra value for the money.

So what kinds of products are baby-boomers interested in? Quite a variety, including the following:

Leisure-time activity products
Fitness and health items
Electronics
Money and financial management products
Home-environment items

BE SUSPICIOUS OF MAILING LISTS

It's wise to be suspicious of mailing lists until you have some substantial proof that their quality is good. With mailing lists selling for such high prices, and with so many lists on the market, there's a lot of competition among mailing-list brokers. This competition sometimes results in deceptive sales practices. If you don't know much about the list company, you can waste a lot of money on poor-quality names, old names passed off as new ones, names that are unsuitable for your offers, and even on lists that have nothing to do with mail-order buyers.

So ask the mailing-list companies you're considering for full details on their lists, and check out each company's reputation in the mail-order business.

Test a list with a relatively small number of names. Another good test is to send your sales letters to more than one mailing list. They may pull well when sent to names on one list and yet do poorly when mailed to another list. A top-quality mailing list is very important for your direct-mail success.

There's one drawback to using lists of mail-order-buyer names. You can probably guess what it is. You have no control over the list of names you rent. You can't be sure the names on the list are fresh, proven mail-order buyers, the right names for the products you have to sell, or even if the addresses are accurate. The only thing you can do is try to deal with responsible list-companies and hope that the information they provide you with is accurate.

You can ask list sources how old the names on their lists are, what types of ads generated the lists, and where the ads appeared. You need to ask such questions in order to find out if a list is any good. You don't want to pay for worthless lists, and there are lots of them floating around. You can get burned if you're not careful. I've stated this warning earlier, but I can't stress it enough. Get all the facts from any list company you're thinking of buying from. If the company won't answer your questions about its lists, try another company.

A number of list companies claim their names are "hot-line." By this, they mean the names on a list belong to people who have recently bought something and are not simply the names of people who were sent free samples of magazines or some type of introductory offer.

One question you definitely need the answer to when considering which list company to buy from, is this: Are lists available for the items you are selling? If not, you're wasting your money. It's important to match your products and services to the right list of buyer names—people who have bought similar products, and bought them recently.

Remember that the single most valuable and important list you have is the list of customers who have sent orders to your company. Guard that list carefully and keep it growing. It can be worth a lot of money to you in the future.

STICK WITH PROVEN MAIL-ORDER PUBLICATIONS

The chances of your ads doing well for you, and bringing in a profit, are far better if you stick with tried-and-proven mail-order publications, such as the following:

Income Opportunities
House Beautiful (which has a special mail-order section)
Popular Mechanics
The Wall Street Journal
Popular Science
Outdoor Life
Small Business Opportunities
Entrepreneur
The Star
Opportunity
Capper's
Wealth Secrets Magazine
Moneysworth
Grit
New Business Opportunities
Fate
Rags to Riches

Sports Afield
The National Enquirer

When you make insertion orders for ads in monthly publications, there's a period of time before your ads appear. Most monthly magazines require that your insertion orders be received anywhere from two to three months before the issue in which your ad will be published. Don't forget about this time lag.

I suggest that you occasionally run ads in the mail-order sections of large Sunday newspapers like the *Chicago Tribune, Atlanta Constitution, Kansas City Star, Los Angeles Times,* and others. Ads run in these weeklies can give you a fast response to your ads. Weekly newspaper ads bring in orders and inquiries within days. If your test ad in a large weekly brings positive results, then you have a much faster indication that your ad may be a winner. This way you won't have to wait several months to learn if your ad produces results.

A SPECIAL WAY TO ADVERTISE

A special company in Sarasota, Florida, handles classified ads for a great many mail-order dealers, doing the job of placing ads for them in well-known mail-order publications. The company is called National Mail-Order Classified. The company has been in business for many years and offers some super advertising bargains. It will run your display and classified ads in combinations of mail-order publications or in magazines and newspapers known for good mail-order results. One special ad-insertion offer made by National Mail-Order Classified allows you to reach a whopping 65-million circulation. That figure is reached by adding the circulations of all the publications in which the company places ads. The current price of this ''Big Jackpot,'' as National Mail-Order Classified calls it, is $55 a word for a ten-word-minimum ad, for a minimum cost of $550 per ad. This gives you a classified ad in a huge group of National's ''Best by Mail'' columns. (Keep in mind that ad prices are subject to increase.)

This does not mean that upwards of 65 million will actually see your ad. But of that total, an enormous number should see it. If your ad has appeal and arouses enough curiosity, it could bring in a tremendous flow of orders or inquiries. The address of National Mail-Order Classified is

National Mail-Order Classified
Post Office Box 5
Sarasota, Florida 34230

The address of National Mail-Order Classified's general headquarters is

National Mail-Order Classified
2628 17th Street
Sarasota, Florida 34230
Phone: (813) 366–3003

(Though you should bear in mind that addresses and phone numbers change, this company has been at the same Sarasota address for many years.)

Without spending too much, you could run a test ad through National Mail-Order Classified. Look over the various bargain specials the firm offers. Write to the company and request a packet of free information. You'll receive a package of circulars and flyers explaining all of National's terrific advertising opportunities. I just sent them an order for several ads myself, and I expect good results.

DON'T JUMP INTO DIRECT MAIL TOO SOON

Again, unless you're a skilled mail-order operator with some solid experience in the business behind you, don't move into direct mail too quickly. Learn as much as possible about classified and small display ads first. Making wrong decisions in direct mail would waste money that could otherwise have been used for classified and space ads. As I've repeatedly stated, obtaining a strong, quality mailing list of prospect names is sometimes hard to do. Many mail-order firms are never quite certain about the degree of quality of the lists they rent.

With more experience in the business, you'll have a chance to learn more about direct mail and be able to decide if some of your offers are right for it. Even a direct-mail test will take time,

THE DIRECT-MAIL PACKAGE

A direct-mail package usually consists of an outer envelope, sales letter, circular, order form, and reply envelope. Of all the package's elements, the sales letter is by far the most important.

especially if you do all your own envelope-stuffing yourself. Sealing and stamping 5,000, 10,000, or more direct-mail letters takes more time than you might think.

After you've gained enough confidence and experience, direct mail could well become your road to spectacular profits. But success takes the right combination of the following factors:

- The right mailing list
- The right product and service offers
- A dynamic, magnetic, compelling sales letter
- A powerful circular, preferably with a picture of the product in use and a description of its main features
- An order form (as part of the sales letter or separate) with clear instructions for sending payment

OVERSTOCK AT YOUR PERIL

I also want to warn you again about overstocking. The way to avoid this pitfall is to test, test, and test again. If the results of your test ads keep turning out poorly, it's usually unwise to proceed any further. But before you reach a completely negative conclusion on a particular offer, try different copy approaches, different headlines, and fresh descriptions. Make sure you've tested thoroughly before ruling out a particular item.

It goes without saying that if test results are consistently negative, you shouldn't stock that item. Overstocking is an error that drives many mail-order operators out of the industry. So I repeat, don't let it happen to you. Make sure, or as reasonably sure as you can, that you have a winner before you pile up too much stock of an item.

RESULT-GETTING GUIDELINES FOR DIRECT-MAIL

1. Put a brief but unusual message on the outside of the envelope.
2. Offer customers and prospects special bonuses and savings.
3. Try a "see through" window envelope occasionally.
4. Definitely use a P.S. on every sales letter you mail. A P.S. commands attention.
5. Include a second offer in the same package.
6. Using credit card charges will increase your sales.
7. Respond to inquiries without delay.
8. Try to use stimulating phrases or questions to entice a customer to open your envelope.
9. Always include a return envelope.
10. Repeat your guarantee and state it effectively.
11. Vary the list sources you use and always be on the lookout for better ones.
12. Use headlines that highlight the top features of your offers.
13. Thank your customers for their business. Show your appreciation.
14. If you offer free gifts, make sure they're free.
15. Try novelty and/or illustrated letterheads occasionally.
16. Handwrite the person's first name in place of "Dear Friend" or "Dear Customer."
17. Cultivate the printers you use. Always have a backup printer on hand.
18. Establish a personality and style for your company.
19. Ask customers what they think of your products and offers.
20. Make your catalog special and different.
21. Make the wording of your offers as dramatic as possible.
22. Time your mailings so they don't arrive on Mondays.
23. Let the customer know if there will be a delay in filling the order.
24. Look for new items and offers to add to your line.
25. Limit the time period for response to your offers.

Some mail-order firms won't even stock an item until they have solid proof that the product is going to sell well enough for them to make a decent profit. Others keep a very low amount of stock on hand, but they have arrangements in place to get more of the item if needed. If you must have stock on hand for a fairly new item, keep it on the low side at first. Don't get overconfident and then get stuck holding the bag.

In mail-order, using common sense pays off. Test in a small way, then see if additional tests confirm the first results. Once you have solid evidence that your item is a winner in the market you're after you can forge ahead. Happiness, for a mail-order company, is selling all the stock of an item. Empty stockrooms are a joy. They mean you're doing something—or everything—right. An empty stockroom usually means a full bank account.

THE FINE LINE BETWEEN PIE-IN-THE-SKY AND FRAUD

Some of the new offers you plan and develop may be money-making plans and programs. If so, I want to caution you regarding the fine line between glitzy, pie-in-the-sky, claims and outright fraud. This fine line is like a tightrope stretched over a dangerous canyon.

Some advertisers stray at will across this line between fantastic-sounding claims and pure fraud. When an ad makes it sound as if it's a foregone conclusion that a buyer will be a millionaire several weeks or months after sending in an order, that is skirting the border between pie-in-the-sky and outright fraud.

Don't risk the future of your company, and what could become a very profitable mail-order career, with fantastic, too-good-to-be-true statements or promises in your ads. This advice is very important for the 1990s, as the postal authorities are cracking down on an increasing number of those who run fraudulent ads.

The bad thing about mail-order fraud is that it hurts the honest companies in the business. More than 145,000 complaints of mail fraud were received by the U.S. Postal Service in a single year. The main complaints were

1. Requests for refunds were not honored
2. Items were never received
3. Orders arrived in damaged condition

4. Orders turned out to be a far cry from what they were advertised to be

Chain letters are illegal, but they have been increasing in recent years. Postal authorities say that "any chain letter which seeks something of value may be a violation of the federal lottery or mail fraud statutes." If a chain letter seeks to circulate things of no value—such as a recipe—it is entirely legal. While some chain letters operate on the fringe of legality (even though they are rip-offs), there's no doubt that most chain-letter schemes hurt the reputation of the mail-order industry. I know of one major newspaper in the South that absolutely refuses to accept mail-order ads of any kind for its Sunday edition, which is the one that reaches the most readers, because it associates mail-order with fraudulent chain-letter schemes. I advise you to avoid chain letters like the plague. Don't ever lend your name, or your company's, to them.

Some people never change. The years go by, but they keep on falling for the same old con deals, including the following:

- Blind phony ads for products that are never sent
- Phony work-at-home deals (some work-at-home schemes, however, are honest)
- Illegal pyramid schemes
- Phony correspondence schools
- Fake invoices for items that were never ordered

So many quality items can be sold by mail—items that are legitimate, useful, and of interest and value—that it's stupid, in my opinion, for mail-order operators ever to get involved with borderline or truly fraudulent ads, sales letters, or products.

The pages of this book contain hundreds of attractive, legitimate ideas for products and services you can consider selling by mail. Try adding any one, or several, to your existing line of items.

I trust you will agree with me in my long-held belief that all the success and money in the world are no good unless a person can come by them honestly and honorably. Human beings have to be able to look at themselves in the mirror each day, sleep at night, and live with themselves.

Your quality offers, backed with effective and persuasive advertising, can and will bring new luster to the mail-order industry. And one day you may be able to look back at decades of quality mail-order service and impressive profits and success. Go for it.

Mail-Order Dynamics for the 1990s

This decade of the 1990s will be gone before we know it, and we'll be in a new century. I predict that, on the whole, the 1990s will be an even more prosperous period of growth for the mail-order industry than the 1980s. Mail-order markets are expanding. More potential customers are waiting out there than ever before. For the mail-order company prepared to offer them quality products and services, the sky really is the limit.

Will your mail-order company become a high achiever by the turn of the new century? The potential is certainly there. Just the fact that you're in a boom industry is a big plus. There's no end to the horizon for this multi-billion-dollar business. I see no reason why you can't get your share (and then some) of this rich mail-order boom.

WHAT MAKES A MAIL-ORDER COMPANY A SUPER-ACHIEVER?

Have you ever wondered what makes some companies super-successful while others seem just to get by or even to fall by the wayside? I've studied, interviewed, and thought on the subject a lot, and I believe certain specific elements play a vital role in a company's rise to the pinnacle of success. I want to share these with you, discussing each in turn.

1. Successful entrepreneurs have a strong basic need to achieve. This need is the fuel-power behind their rise to spectacular success. As I put it in an earlier chapter, these people "fan the flame of their desire" to go places in business, to grow, to arrive on the success scene. When they hear other success stories, they focus more energy on making their own success unfold. They devote a lot of time and attention to this need to achieve, and the effort pays off handsomely.

2. High achievers are optimistic about the future. Talk to these achievers or read about their careers, and this one similarity comes across.

Some people downplay optimism's importance, but the facts say otherwise. Throughout history, waves of optimism have risen time and again and led people and nations to success. The founding fathers of the United States had it: a great feeling of hope for America's future.

If optimism is the feeling or practice of thinking that "every day in every way, you're getting better and better," what could possibly be wrong with that? The business owners who think in this way usually do get better and better, and so do their companies.

3. Super-achievers cultivate the ability to see and act on a profit opportunity. The key element is simply the vision to foresee profit in a given opportunity and the will to act on that vision. If you are already running a mail-order company, then you no doubt possess this trait. You wouldn't have started a mail-order company unless you believed there was money to be made in the business—and lots of it. Others see the chance for profit, but they fail to act on it. You acted. You followed through on it by launching your mail-order firm. Where would Joe

SUCCESS STORY
SONGWRITING GUIDE

Whaen I first began to run my own mail-order business, I discovered through research that a whopping 35 million people in the United States write songs and are trying to sell them to music publishers or recording companies. Millions more all over the world are caught up in the lure of a music career. I knew songwriting well, having had a number of my own songs recorded and performed. With my experience in the field, I knew I could develop some helpful material for songwriters. So I spent several months developing a songwriting guide.

I used the inquiry-and-follow-up advertising method to get prospects. I ran classified ads in the leading mail-order publications and then sent full information on my music career guide to those who responded. My first few ads brought an avalanche of requests for more details. I quickly sold out of my first printing of the guide. I still sell it today, for $14.95 per copy, and it continues to bring in cash orders and inquiries through classified ads and direct mail. There's a huge market out there for informational, how-to guides. Go for it!

Karbo or the founders of L. L. Bean, Sears, and other stars of the industry have gone if they had passed up their opportunities and not acted on them? The answer is obvious.

4. Top achievers have an abundance of energy. They're willing to work 60- and 70-hour workweeks, if necessary, to achieve their goals. This is especially true when they first launch their companies and during their businesses' early years.

5. They thrive on competition. Competition is not seen as a bad thing by high achievers. Nor is it viewed as a threat to their own companies. On the contrary, they learn from competing companies and believe that the competition keeps them on their toes. Most believe that a competitive spirit is the backbone of the free enterprise system.

6. People at the top of their professions exhibit a strong degree of self-confidence. High achievers of the world are not timid, downcast, or depressed persons. They have a lot of faith

in themselves, their talents, and their companies. In fact, quite a few of them reek of self-confidence. They generally agree with the spirit and philosophy of General George Patton: "Always do your best. In the long run, that's the most important thing." Their confidence is a daily ally and source of strength. They march straight ahead in the direction of their dreams.

7. They have the knack of developing items that sell. We've seen how important effective advertising is in mail-order, but one major reason for the big success of high achievers is this "sixth sense" for coming up with offers that mail-order buyers want. When attractive products are matched up with strong advertising, the results are often substantial profits.

8. High achievers don't rest on their laurels. They are forever seeking a broader horizon, more profits, and a higher sales volume. They're not long content once they've met a particular goal. They immediately set up new goals to strive for. Some treat it as a game, but one with serious stakes involved. They seem to thrive on constant challenge. It keeps them motivated and dedicated to continuous advancement for their companies.

KNOW THE TOTAL MARKETING PICTURE FOR THE 1990s

You should be aware of what is meant by the "total marketing picture." It means all the various factors that must be taken into consideration when planning and applying a marketing strategy for a particular product or service. The total marketing picture includes the following:

- Packaging
- Advertising
- Promotion
- Merchandising
- Selling

The two areas you'll use most in mail-order are advertising and promotion, but of course the whole objective of your strategy is to sell the product, so selling is at the heart of the total picture.

All the areas are meant to work together to sell the product. By coordinating these five phases of your work and seeing that each is handled as well as possible, you will improve your chances of making larger profits on what you sell by mail.

Factors that will affect your marketing picture throughout the 1990s include the following:

1. New, effective packaging ideas will come out frequently.
2. Advertising will center more around the universal wants such as the desire for security, recognition, and success.
3. Fresh new promotional and merchandising ideas will play a large role in the marketing picture.
4. Learning systems will be modernized and sales-management skills streamlined.

Effective new sales tools will lead to an exploration of new markets. Each new decade brings ever-more efficient sales tools and new markets for those tools to exploit.

YOU CAN ALWAYS FALL BACK ON CLASSIFIEDS

The following guide will be useful in helping you to determine if you should sell an item directly from a classified ad.

1. Does the item you wish to sell sound like a bargain? If so, can you get this idea across in a few well-chosen words?
2. Is the item low-priced (from about $5.00 to $10.00)? Many mail-order operators feel that $10.00 is too much to ask for directly from an ad. They believe a sales letter is necessary when an item costs $10.00 or more. If you agree, you should use classified ads to draw inquiries about an item, then send interested prospects a sales letter in which you ask for their money.
3. Does your item offer genuine value that will leave your customers satisfied?
4. Is the item something people need? Often, repeat-sale items such as address labels, office supplies, printing services, and similar products and services are right for

classifieds. But it's harder to establish an item that must be ordered again and again.

5. Will many prospects be interested in the item? If the offer is too specialized, you will be better off not trying to sell it from an ad.

If you can answer yes to the five questions above, you probably have an item that can be successfully sold directly from an ad.

PROJECTING FUTURE GOALS AND PRODUCTS

Steve Brennan, a former teacher and athletic coach, started his own business at age 38. He summarizes what it took to get started and to plan his future goals in this way: "I expected to have some tough building years before I would be competitive. I was starting from scratch. You have to develop mental toughness. I knew I'd have to work hard. I knew I would need a positive attitude. You need to get pumped up, set goals, be highly motivated. Confidence is all important in developing a winning attitude." If there's one single word that's all-important for your future in mail-order, that word has to be "planning."

If you make up your mind today that you want your mail-order company to double its profits in the next year or two, then start at once to plan how you can accomplish this goal. Actually write down your goals for the next few years. Decide where you would like to be in the first year of the new century.

As you make progress toward your goals, be sure to be mindful of how your success happened and continue to plan at regular intervals. As for products, remember that just because one or two items don't click, it doesn't mean you have no future in mail-order. You're not down the drain. You simply need to go back to the drawing board and come up with other ideas. It may take a number of duds before you have a product or service that makes it. So what? The point is that you don't give up or get discouraged when one or two items fail to live up to your expectations.

One of the greatest things about the mail-order business is that you can always try another product or service. The next one might well be the one that puts you on the road to success.

When you decide that it's time to double your profits, be sure to give yourself a realistic amount of time to achieve the goal. You might set a goal of doubling your profits in six months or a year. Some mail-order operators might prefer to accomplish this in even less time.

If you're now selling just one item, you may want to add three or four items to your line during the next year. It's strictly up to you. You may prefer to stay a small company, focusing mainly on classified and small display ads and never venture into direct mail. Or you may eventually try your hand at all three.

Remember that mail-order is a business of *products*. So saturate your mind with old products, new products, any products. Services, too. Time spent thinking about products is never wasted. Take the time to research old products. Look at mail-order publications of ten, 20, or more years ago. What was selling well then? Sometimes bringing back an old product is a highly profitable move.

A new product or service idea may be forming in your mind at any time. That's natural for an entrepreneur like you. Any one of your ideas could develop into a blockbuster and make a fortune. There's always that potential.

Try to focus on its key characteristics when you have a new mail-order product in mind. Use the following list of characteristics as a guide for comparing your product idea with competing items:

1. Size and weight
2. Price
3. Appearance and style
4. Durability
5. Versatility
6. Convenience
7. Accuracy or speed
8. Usefulness
9. Installation cost

YOUR PROJECTED SALES VOLUME

There's power in expectation, so you should set sales volume goals for your mail-order company. When you start a new year, ask yourself what your sales volume should be for the year. Here is a good way to record these sales goals.

First Year	First Product	Second Product	Total Sales
	$_____	$_____	$_____
Units	_____	_____	_____
Second Year	$_____	$_____	$_____
Units	_____	_____	_____

MAIL-ORDER AT THE TURN OF THE CENTURY

What will the mail-order industry be like at the turn of the century, and beyond? Here are my own predictions.

1. I believe there will be even more demand for information products and services. In his book *Megatrends*, author John Naisbitt emphasizes the fact that information is our most valuable resource. We live today in an "information society," and I believe this trend will intensify during the decade.

If you offer information through books, manuals, booklets, or folios, and you advertise these products effectively, your business should continue to do well into the twenty-first century.

In his excellent book *Secrets of a Freelance Writer (How to Make $85,000 a Year)*, Robert Bly tells how he used mail-order to land clients for his commercial business-writing company. As Bly puts it, "If you're someone who can create, package, and market information—the twilight of the twentieth century represents a time of almost unlimited profit opportunity for you." I strongly recommend that you add his book to your reading list. It's bound to help you as you build your company.

2. More programs, plans, manuals, ideas, and information packages will be sold in the form of cassette tapes. What is offered today as a ten-dollar book or manual will be put on a cassette and sold for $39.95 by the turn of the century. In fact, this is already happening, but the practice will become even more widespread by the year 2000. One company that now offers a real-estate opportunity program on cassette originally sold it as a $10 book. And sales of the tape-recorded cassette are strong.

3. More mail-order advertising will be done on cable TV, as well as on regular broadcast television. One company, for example, now advertises a caffeine pill to help women lose weight. The company runs its ads on cable television, and buyers can place orders by calling a toll-free telephone number. The company uses no print ads and sends out no sales letters. The cable television commercials do it all. At last report, this company was receiving thousands of orders.

Today you are seeing the beginning of a cable TV boom that shows no signs of leveling off. If you can pay for cable television commercials for your products, you'll find yourself in the big time. You'll be swamped with so many orders you'll probably have to hire your neighbors, friends, and family members to help you fill them all.

4. Money-making plans, programs, and systems will be in even greater demand, and the ads for them will become more sophisticated. There will be fewer gimmicks and ''sob stories'' about how the advertiser was down to his last dollar when a brilliant idea that led him to riches suddenly came to him. Customers are becoming much more knowledgeable, demanding, and harder to please, and this trend will continue into the next century. They'll be much more likely not to fall for gimmicks and unworkable schemes. Instead, they'll be looking for genuine value for their money, and they'll expect and demand higher quality products.

5. Mail-order will be increasingly used as a way of obtaining business-to-business clients. More businesses will have discovered what an effective tool mail-order is in generating inquiries from companies interested in a variety of business products and services. So more businesses will use mail-order

to get inquiries and then turn over the leads to their sales teams.

6. The headlines, copy, and total effect of ads will be more persuasive, appealing, and powerful. They'll have to be to compete with other ads and keep pulling in orders.

7. There will be an explosion in the number of new mail-order (including catalog) companies. The industry will have grown by leaps and bounds by the turn of the century, and it will be poised for even more dramatic growth in the early years of the new century.

8. The mail-order market will be absolutely enormous. A huge number of people will be seeking a better life—and better products and services—from mail-order. I predict the turn of the century will be a magnificent time to be an established mail-order company with a growing line of items that people want to buy. Even poor economic periods and times of recession have little effect on mail-order buying. In fact, many products sell even more strongly at such times.

The profits, success, and achievement you want are all within the mail-order industry. Chart the course to your desired destination now.

Over many years, I have studied the similarities among people who have made their dreams come true, whether they were dreams of wealth, business success, fame, or whatever. All of them fanned the flame of their desire, and here are the key ways they did it:

- Most had a big dream to start with—something they were determined to bring to reality.
- Most refused to heed the doubts, warnings, and skepticism of others who said they could never have the dream they wanted.
- They thought about their dream every day and did something to keep moving closer to it.
- All refused to give up when temporary setbacks came their way. They focused on the dream and bounced back quickly.
- They did not abandon their dream—not even when devastating misfortune and disaster struck them.

- Most had faith that they could attain their dream. And they asked for God's help and guidance.
- Many were more than willing to "pay their dues" over the years in order to be qualified to fulfill their dream.
- They stuck to the pursuit of their dream until it became a reality. They were not wishy-washy, hopping from one dream to another. They had the courage of their convictions.
- Most of them sooner or later devised strategic plans of action to help them move closer to their dream.

Benjamin Franklin once contributed his own definition of happiness: "Human happiness is produced not so much by great pieces of good fortune that seldom happen, as by little advantages that occur every day." Watch for those little advantages that occur every day in your mail-order business.

Boom times are great times to profit, if you act in advance and are ready for them. I believe you can be a part of the great boom era ahead for the mail-order industry. If only a few of the products and services that you bring into the lives of others help them, inform them, make their lives easier, more comfortable, safer, more profitable, happier, and more interesting, then your company's existence will have been more than justified. Offer products that really enrich the lives of your customers, and I predict you'll go far in mail-order.

It is my sincere wish that this book, along with my first book on mail-order, *Money In Your Mailbox* (New York, John Wiley & Sons, 1985), will guide, help, and inspire you to attain substantial profits and success throughout the 1990s, and beyond. I'll be seeing you out there in the fascinating world of mail-order. And may your mailbox stay filled with orders far into the twenty-first century.

Mail-Order Products That Usually Sell Well

Talking balloons.   This product is currently selling very well. One company in Georgia has its phones ringing off the hook after ads for the product appear.

Cassette tapes and records that give instruction.   One company did well offering a self-hypnosis tape. Other types of instructional material can be put on cassettes and sold at a big profit.

Mailbox covers.   You see ads for this product in the mail-order-shopping pages of *House Beautiful* magazine.

Pet products.   Pets are often treated better than many human beings. So be alert for pet-oriented products you could offer by mail. There's an enormous market here. Some items that have sold well are dog collars, toys for pets, pet certificates, and clothing items for pets.

Home-study courses.   These do not have to be complicated or lengthy correspondence courses. You could offer any number of home-study materials on becoming a money broker or piano tuner, how to write filler material, public speaking, and many other subjects.

Menu services.   Plan menus for several or more months into the future and sell them by mail. One woman in the Midwest reportedly earns more than $75,000 a year selling her menu service by mail.

Magnifying eyeglasses.   This item has sold well for years and continues to do so. The product can be sold year-round and also as a gift item. It might help if you could make the item somehow better, or different, from that offered by competing firms.

Money-making plans, manuals, programs, systems, and ideas.
These have been some of the largest producers of fortunes in the mail-order industry. They're often sold via half-page and full-page ads in leading opportunity magazines. Many of them are also sold in smaller display ads or using the inquiry-and-follow-up-method via classified ads.

Novelty items.   Magic tricks, jokes, and a variety of handmade and imported products are good examples. The Pet Rock made a huge fortune for its creator. Try to come up with something that would have mass appeal.

Baby items.   The millions of families with babies could keep a supply of orders coming your way for years to come.

Bridal items.   It's possible to offer all manner of gifts for weddings, engagements, and bridal showers.

Toys and games.   These items have been sold by mail-order since the earliest days of the industry. Christmas is the best time for them, but with effective ads they can sell throughout the year.

Dolls.   Some mail-order companies have done amazingly well selling unique, inexpensive dolls.

Theft alarms in cars.   Two million car alarms were sold in 1989. The best prospects are people who have already had a break-in. Sales should continue to rise twenty percent a year.

Art supplies.   Buying by mail is an easy and inexpensive way to obtain art supplies. With the millions of amateur artists out there, this could be a long-term, continuous market for you.

Flags.   This item might have a big upsurge in sales, with all the flap about the American Flag being desecrated. Getting flags produced might be troublesome. But there is no question that sales are up.

Many U.S. citizens were outraged at what they perceived as the mistreatment of the flag. I would label this item as a "possible."

Cosmetics. Working women form a gigantic market. The hottest current sellers in the cosmetics trade are "ethnic" products, hair-care products, and skin preparations. Total U.S. cosmetics sales were $17.5 billion in 1989.

Here are some other products you might consider offering:

Coin banks
Curtains
Exercise aids
Puzzles
Household inventory
    books
Boutique items

Family crest rings
Patent information for
    Inventors
Porcelain plates
Self-defense products
Camping and recreation
    items

Address Sources for Building Your Business

Small Business Administration
1441 L Street, N.W.
Washington, D.C. 20416

Ask for their pamphlet "Selling by Mail-Order."

The Stationery House, Inc.
1000 Florida Avenue
Hagerstown, Maryland 21741

This company occasionally offers bargain prices on business envelopes (printing).

Superintendent of Documents
U.S. Government Printing House
Washington, D.C. 20402

Ask to be put on the agency's free mailing list. You will be sent information on all the new materials the Government Printing House publishes.

Champion Printing Company
Box 148
Ross, Ohio 45061

Note: All addresses are subject to change.

A Sample Classified Order and Advertising Contract

The following pages show an ad insertion order form and a typical advertising contract.

Classified Advertising Order

NATIONAL MAIL ORDER CLASSIFIED
P.O. BOX 5 — SARASOTA, FL 34230

"Money in the Bank" Classifieds That Pull Month After Month

Name _____

Address _____

City/State/Zip _____

Please rush insertion of our ad in your next National Mail Order Classified "Best By Mail" column in the next available issue of magazines listed below.

_____   _____

_____   TOTAL ORDER AMOUNT_____

PLEASE CHECK THESE CONDITIONS WHEN ORDERING

5% discount on 3 or more insertions in same publication or group. Fill in copy in spaces below or use any paper if order blank is spoiled or more space is needed for more words. Closing for most magazines is the 15th, but ads should be sent in at once so a repro of your ad can be sent to you if possible, before the final deadline. Most tabloids and newspapers close weekly. We reserve the right to reject ads not acceptable to publishers. In the event an ad is rejected by a publication, equal or better value will be made up in other accepting publications. Money is refunded if ad cannot be placed anywhere. Advertising non-cancellable. Not responsible for client errors in copy sent to us or for any legal actions resulting from such errors or any claims made by advertisers. Copies of columns including your ad as sent to publishers are also sent to you after each closing. Renewal Notices are sent with ample time allowed so you won't miss any issues. We keep you informed all the way! All taxes included.

MINIMUM 10 WORDS - PAYMENT WITH ORDER PLEASE

ADVERTISING COPY

1	2	3	4	5
6	7	8	9	10
11	12	13	14	15
16	17	18	19	20
21	22	23	24	25
26	27	28	29	30
31	32	33	34	35

- Please use any blank sheet if you have more than 35 words in your classified, or if you need more space to list publications in which you wish your ad to appear.
- If you wish all bold letters in the first line of your classified for extra attention, add the cost of 2 words to your payment. Please check box at left.
- Available: Top 3 positions under "Best By Mail" headings. Add 10% of classified cost.

NM-188
67

Display Advertising Order

NATIONAL MAIL ORDER CLASSIFIED

P.O. BOX 5 — SARASOTA, FL 34230

No charge for setting display ads. One time charge of $15. for making cut if illustration is needed. See display ad sheet.

Name _____

Address _____

City/State/Zip _____

Please rush insertion of our ad in your next National Mail Order Classified "Best By Mail" column in the next available issue of magazines listed below

_____   _____

_____   TOTAL ORDER AMOUNT _____

PLEASE CHECK THESE CONDITIONS WHEN ORDERING

5% discount on 3 or more insertions in same publication or group. Fill in copy in spaces below or use any paper if order blank is spoiled or, more space is needed for more words. Closing for most magazines is the 15th, but ads should be sent in at once so a repro of your ad can be sent to you, if possible, before the final deadline. Most tabloids and newspapers close weekly. We reserve the right to reject ads not acceptable to publishers. In the event an ad is rejected by a publication, equal or better value will be made up in other accepting publications. Money is refunded if ad cannot be placed anywhere. Advertising non-cancellable. Not responsible for client errors in copy sent to us or for any legal actions resulting from such errors or any claims made by advertisers. Copies of columns including your ad as sent to publishers are also sent to you after each closing. Renewal Notices are sent with ample time allowed so you won't miss any issues. We keep you informed all the way!

ADVERTISING COPY

Please use any blank sheet if you need more space to list publications in which you wish to advertise or need a larger sheet for your display advertising layout.

Advertising Contract

AGENCY/ADVERTISER:

Company: _____
Address: _____
_____
Attention: _____
Phone: _____

ADVERTISING INSERTION ORDER FOR: (USE ONE INSERTION ORDER PER PUBLICATION)

☐ Successful Opportunities
☐ Wealth Secrets   (CHECK ONE ONLY)

INCLUSIVE DATE(S): _____ On Sale _____ Closing Date _____
ISSUE DATE (mo./yr.)

AD DESCRIPTION:

Size ___ _____ Color _____ Key _____

RATE (Gross) = _____ Less 15% Commission _____ Less 2% discount = _____ Net.
(Above allowed only on pre-paid ads or invoices paid within 10 days of receipt)

TERMS: Pre-payment required for non-established accounts. Payable upon publication, net due 30 days—15% commission allowed to recognized agencies—Invoices must be paid within 30 day billing term to qualify—Additional 2% discount if paid within 10 days of invoice. These terms apply to display ads only. Classified ads are non-commissionable. Please note contract conditions below.

ADDITIONAL INSTRUCTIONS: _____
_____
_____

Authorized Signature _____ Date _____

Please sign and return white copy to our offices, it must be received by the closing date to assure publication.

CONTRACT CONDITIONS: This contract is with the named firm/individual (advertiser) and change of ownership or management will not dissolve contract obligations. All charges are due and payable as stated herein. Advertiser and agent (if any) agrees to be responsible for payment thereof. In any action brought upon this agreement, venue shall be proper in San Diego, California, and advertiser and agent expressly waive any objections to venue or personal jurisdiction therein. All advertisements are placed solely at the risk of the advertiser/agency. The publisher does not in anyway guarantee any level of advertising results and is not in any way responsible for those results.

National Publications Inc.

6150 Mission Gorge Rd., Suite 225 • San Diego, CA 92120 • (619) 280-5800

Copywriting as an Art and a Business

To be a copywriter is to be in the front ranks of the business world. Advertising copywriters move the goods and products of a nation. Whether they work for large or small advertisers or for an advertising agency, good copywriters are treasured by their employers. One successful copywriter put it this way: "I write the ads and commercials that stimulate the economy and keep my country moving forward. And I'm well paid for doing it." Not a bad way to spend your energy.

Elmer Wheeler, affectionately known as the dean of American salesmen, once summed up the work of a copywriter most effectively: "The best-looking merchandise won't sell . . . without the intelligent persuasion of somebody's words." It's often been said that copywriting is "salesmanship in print." It takes a good copywriter to conceive of words and ideas that sell goods and services.

A number of copywriters in today's business world pull in more than $75,000 a year. Those at the top take home well over

$100,000 each year, plus profit-sharing, bonuses, and other perks. A man or woman with proven ability to write selling ads can often write his or her own ticket. The huge demand for outstanding copywriters is illustrated by this story:

Not long ago, a woman with very little copywriting experience landed a copy spot with a New York ad agency at a starting salary of $70,000. A company specializing in the placement of copywriters and other advertising talent obtained the job for her. The better and more experienced a copywriter is, the higher the financial rewards may be. Even average copywriters are doing well and can go far in the industry.

A SCARCITY OF NEW TALENT

Jerry Fields, Managing Director of Jerry Fields Associates in New York, has emphasized the lack of advertising copywriting talent available in recent years: ''There is an almost devastating scarcity of new, fresh copy talent.'' This lack has resulted in the same veteran writers being recycled at larger and larger salaries. Unlike a number of other occupations, the older a good copywriter gets—at least with the current situation—the more money he or she can earn.

HOW MANY COPYWRITERS MAKE THEIR START

A lot of copywriters get their initial start in the business by going to work for department stores. Look in on the offices of many department stores and speciality shops, and you're likely to find busy copywriters getting the current ads written and out. Copywriting for stores is still a good stepping-stone to higher-paying spots with either advertising agencies or major companies that do their own advertising.

WHY COPYWRITING IS AN ART

Perhaps the main reason that copywriting will always be an art is simply that there are so many different ways to sing the praises of a product or service, underscoring its special qualities, usefulness, and benefits. Every veteran copywriter knows this basic truth and keeps it in mind in his or her daily work.

The copywriter's target is always the same: to highlight in an unforgettable way the key advantage of a given product. The art comes into play in how this is actually accomplished. There are numerous ways to be persuasive with words, pictures, and sounds.

The copywriter's job is to decide on the best way to spotlight a product's main features. And the product itself holds the clues as to how this can be done. So in a real way the seeds of copywriting success are already there within the existing product. William Bernbach, one of the all-time greats of the industry, said it well: ''The most important element in success in ad writing is the product itself.''

COPYWRITING IS ALSO A BUSINESS

There's no doubt that the amount of advertising will continue to grow in the years ahead. As the shorter workweek grows more popular and acceptable, more and more millions of workers will have extra free time and therefore a need for all types of products and services to help them enjoy their leisure.

Private industry started to experiment with the four-day workweek and other alternative work schedules back in the late 1960s. Since the middle of the 1970s, some 3,500 American companies have been on the four-day schedule. The total number of workers involved is over a million. Some are even predicting a shorter 32-hour workweek for many workers in the years ahead.

So it's clear that advertising is a boom industry, for the rest of this fast-fading century at least. And this means that more copywriters will be needed to write the ads and commercials designed to lead consumers to buy things to make their lives more healthy, enjoyable, safe, and productive.

Hobbies alone make up a large industry. And advertising is used to urge hobby enthusiasts to buy all manner of items related to their avocations. A shorter workweek would clearly make it possible for many more millions of workers to pursue a hobby. Hobbies relieve stress and have a way of providing people with a sense of renewal. According to Dr. Anthony Lulie, a leading Argentinian doctor, ''The secret of a long and healthy life is to forget worry, learn to relax, eat sensibly and keep mentally and physically happy.''

ADVERTISING INCREASES SALES AND PROFITS

There's no denying that advertising increases advertisers' overall sales and profits. Companies wouldn't keep advertising if the results were not favorable. Many companies earmark a large chunk of their yearly profits for additional advertising. They know it will pay off in the long run.

Not every company can advertise in large national publications or on network television, but even the local and regional advertising produced by smaller firms is effective to stimulate new sales.

I draw one good example of how advertising can be used to increase sales from my own experience. When I saw the topnotch, highly professional career booklets produced by the insurance company I represented for a number of years—New York Life—I knew at once that here was an ''open sesame'' to many new sales.

New York Life prepared this series of attractive booklets on all kinds of careers and vocations. They were made with young people in mind and are fine study aids for anyone considering a career as a salesman, teacher, doctor, farmer, nurse, or pharmacist. National advertising brought in a huge number of requests for these excellent booklets, and the inquiries received naturally led to an enormous number of new prospect names. Not all of these people turned out to be qualified prospects, of course, but a great many did.

Another example from my own past proves that making good use of advertising can pay off time after time. One day I noticed an unusually strong ad headline, in the form of a question, in a national magazine. My company had placed the full-page ad for the product, which was a special educational program.

I thought the headline was so strong that I decided to try taking a copy of the full-page ad with me on my calls for a week and using it in my approach to prospects. There's no doubt that it helped me land at least six extra sales during that week alone, as well as additional sales in the weeks and months that followed. The copywriter who wrote that particular ad increased my bank balance considerably.

To get effective advertising that will grab the time and attention of busy consumers everywhere, it takes the teamwork of skilled copywriters, artists, art directors, media people, account executives, research departments, production workers, and general office employees.

Advertising is big business, and it's getting bigger all the time. Claude Hopkins, perhaps the most brilliant copywriter and advertising expert of the century, once said something that every copywriter should frame, put over his or her desk, and look at several times a day: ''The only purpose of advertising is to make sales. Money spending is a serious matter. The more you tell the more you sell.''

MOVING AHEAD AS A MAIL-ORDER COPYWRITER

Most copywriters start out with the desire to write good copy. They take satisfaction in seeing their words in print and their commercials on the air. But they also want their ads and commercials to do a strong selling job, for this is the main objective.

I'm a copywriter myself, and have been one for years. I presently serve a number of national clients as an advertising consultant. I've written ads and radio and television commercials for all kinds of products and services. I've also written news releases, promotional material, brochures, catalog sheets, product fliers, and full-length speeches. I'm no stranger to direct-mail and mail-order copy. I proved years ago in my own life that *copy is king*. I discovered long ago, as you no doubt have or soon will, that the greatest thing ever invented in this world is words. Most copywriters love them.

I know your desire to write ads and commercials that get results. I understand your hopes and dreams for the future. I promise you this. Your future as a copywriter can be a very rewarding and successful one. The years ahead look absolutely fantastic for copywriters who know their way around in the industry. The copywriter, man or woman, is the very heart of the ad agency or company advertiser.

One truth about copywriting will do much to keep you enthusiastic and motivated. That truth is the fact that advertising is a business that recognizes and rewards talent quickly. As a skilled copywriter, you can go up the success ladder much faster than you might dream.

The satisfaction, reward, challenge, stimulation, and creativity of copywriting will keep you growing in your work. Your career will come alive as you explore writing for different kinds of media, enhance your love of language, and work with other creative people as part of an advertising team.

Someone once wrote that the person who can persuade can move the world. As a thriving copywriter, you will enjoy a higher standard of living and make it possible for others to do the same. You will create jobs for many others through your writing. Give your best to your copywriting career every day. Create new ads and commercials with dedication and pride. For you belong to a fabulous profession. You're a copywriter. And *copy is king*.

How to Develop a Good Sales Letter

A strong-pulling sales letter is absolutely vital for direct-mail success. Remember, you may have a truly top-notch product or service, but if you can't sell it effectively you will not get orders. Here are some proven steps for developing a good sales letter:

1. Design an effective letterhead. Few prospects will react to a letter printed on plain paper and without a company name and address at the top. Black-and-white letterheads can pull orders, but using one or two colors usually brings better results.
2. Make your letter sound friendly. Cold, lifeless letters go nowhere.
3. Use letter-size (8-1/2 by 11 inch), 20-pound stock paper. Again, colored paper is better than plain white. In my own business, I've found that women prospects respond to pink and men to blue, but there's no hard-

and-fast rule on this. You can test different colors of paper and ink to see what works best.

4. Avoid wordiness and long, involved paragraphs. The best sales letters are inviting to read. Underline words for emphasis and indent paragraphs. Keep the total effect of your letter simple. Orders come from easy-to-read letters.

5. For best results, have your printing done on one side of the paper only. But for a four-page letter, you can hold the paper cost down by printing on both sides of a sheet. Some letters still seem to pull well even when printed on both sides and without any colors. It's what your letter says that counts the most. But do try to keep your letter neat and professional looking.

6. Many good sales letters still open with "Dear Friend." Yours can do the same or you can skip the greeting entirely.

7. Be as specific as possible when explaining your offer.

8. Try to appeal to a prospect's emotions and dominant desires.

9. Remember that a sales letter may run from a single page up to four or even to eight pages. Some of the most powerful sales letters I've seen were eight pages long. This number of pages is often used to sell high-priced items.

10. Use a P.S. at the end of your sales letter. Make this P.S. a strong appeal for action, a reminder of any bonus gift you are offering, or a fresh wrap-up of your offer. Never underestimate the power of a strong P.S. at the close of your letter. An effective P.S. can increase the number of orders you receive.

The following pages present two direct-mail sales letters that have been effective in my own work.

CREATIVE CONCEPTS

814 Waterman Road South
Jacksonville, Florida 32207

THERE'S NEVER BEEN A BETTER TIME TO CREATE AND PROSPER! YOUR CREATIVE IDEAS CAN BUILD YOU A GROWING SECOND INCOME AND MAYBE A FORTUNE !

Hello there, I'm Perry Wilbur.

UNBELIEVABLE as it seems, best-selling novelist Margaret Mitchell, the creator of GONE WITH THE WIND, did not think her book was any good. She accepted only $50,000 for it. Then Hollywood went on to gross over $100 million dollars on it...over the years.

My friend, I hope I've grabbed your attention! Your very own creative ideas could bring you a handsome second income, pay for your new car, glamour vacations, a new home, shopping sprees galore, boats, diamond rings, college for your kids, or any other desires you have that add up to the good life. Your creative ideas could make you rich beyond belief!

Ideas? They keep this old planet turning in space. The better they are, the further they can take you.

I'm talking about ideas for all sorts of creative projects...including games, toys, ads, greeting cards, inventions, songs, food products, short stories, speeches, articles, books, jokes, novels, plays, comedy routines, cartoons, gags, movie ideas, T.V. programs, radio commercials, newsletters, cassettes, cable T.V., new businesses, services for the public, scripts, musical jingles, business reports, booklets, magazines, pamphlets, and more.

I've been happy most of my life because I've been an IDEA PERSON. I love 'em, and they've done a lot for me. They've taken me to all the glittering capitals of the world, into movie studios, introduced me to film stars, celebrities, and VIPs. My ideas have produced fifteen published books (some are best sellers), recorded songs, T.V. scripts, and thousands of published article credits in magazines and newspapers here and in twenty other countries worldwide.

Many of my ideas have paid off for me for years in the form of beautiful CHECKS or royalties that keep flowing in month after month just like clockwork. A number of these ideas have won me national awards and also a seat at banquet tables, my picture in newspapers and magazines, and other recognition. Why do I mention this? I don't wish to sound like I'm bragging. I just want you to know the FRINGE BENEFITS that come from having successful creative ideas. The checks and royalties are great, but the fringe benefits are often very nice too!

I see no reason why you can't do the same and profit handsomely from your own ideas. You would not have read this far unless you're a creative type of person...or someone interested in creativity who enjoys working with ideas.

Frankly, nobody out there has cornered the market on good ideas. Anyone may get a SUPER idea at any time or place. That includes YOU! But the trick is knowing how to be alert for these ideas, how to mine them (like the GOLD they really are), develop the best ones, and go to the stars with them.

I'm so enthused over what I know creative ideas can do for you that I've put my own years of experience and know-how into a special book that is designed to get you into this fascinating idea business. So far, and I say this with pride, not a single person who has ordered my book has returned it. It will stimulate you to start producing ideas FAST!

But I warn you. Being an idea person is very rewarding, satisfying, exciting, and stimulating. Once you get hooked on ideas, you're usually hooked for life. Actor-comedian Steve Allen was hooked from the day his first short poem appeared in a Chicago newspaper.

The price of my book, titled CREATE AND PROSPER, is very reasonable at only $10.00 plus $1.00 to cover the cost of postage and handling. The price will be going up within the next several months so don't miss your chance now to get it for ten dollars. As they say, "It just might be the start of something BIG for you...in the exciting, whacky, but always fascinating idea business. Ideas you have now can be turned into CASH or royalties.

Like they say in the great game of chess, "It's your move." Send in an order today for this book CREATE AND PROSPER. Hitch your wagon NOW to the world of ideas. You'll never be sorry. There's no telling how far your creative ideas might take you. They can send your star soaring. If it can happen to me, it can happen for you too. Remember, sometimes all you need is one BIG idea.

My book will be rushed to you with my ninety-day guarantee. You may return it any time within ninety days for a full and immediate refund.

Good luck, God bless you, and happy thoughts for more super creative ideas. I'll see you out there in the fascinating idea world of tomorrow! Start your own thrilling adventure with creative ideas. Send in your order today!

Send $10.00 CASH-CHECK-MONEY ORDER (Allow two-three weeks for checks to clear.)
NAME (Please print)_____
ADDRESS_____
CITY-STATE-ZIP CODE_____
Please include a dollar bill to cover the cost of postage and handling.

CREATIVE CONCEPTS

814 Waterman Road South
Jacksonville, Florida 32207

Yes, music lover,

your inquiring reply indicates an interest and likely love for
music...and particularly Country Music! Right? Therefore, this
letter to you should hold your attention, excite you about your
future, and arouse your musical ambitions! It describes a
wonderful and fascinating book called "How to Launch Your Career
in Country Music."

As I am the writer-publisher of this book, I hope you'll forgive my
expression of enthusiasm in the enclosed circular which presents
the highlights of my book...the secrets and seven key routes to a
successful career of your very own in Country Music! When you see
and read this amazing book (unique in its field), you will
understand why I am proud of it.

What does the title mean? It means that inside the book you will find
clear-cut, specific directions on how to find a place for yourself
in the glittering world of Country Music! How to make a start as a
singer, songwriter, performer, musician, or behind-the-scenes
person is spelled out for you. You can use this information to
establish yourself in a rewarding music career.

It may be that some other phase of the music business interests you.
Perhaps you want to become a publishing executive, an arranger, a
country or general music disk-jockey in a radio station, a country
performer on T.V., a promoter of singers, or someone who works in
the business offices (the administrative end) of a music publishing
company or recording label.

You will learn what the different areas of the field are and discover the
career possibilities. To get somewhere in Country Music, you need
to know how to make important contacts, how to write and sell
the kind of country songs that have the BEST chances of becoming
HITS, how to sell your songs by mail, find a partner to write songs
with (in case you write only words or music yourself), how to
analyze the style of big-name appeal singers, and special other
streamlined career pointers to keep you moving up in the music
business.

If you write songs, you'll find extra special information on your choice of song performance rights organizations, how to get your first song accepted and recorded, a must-do for every song you write, the importance of ASCAP and BMI, what to look for when signing song contracts, your first radio announcing or DJ job, how major country stars made it to the top, and what music trade publications you should read regularly.

If you've ever thought about forming your own act, or musical group, to perform or record the songs you and your group create yourselves, then you NEED this book!

All the action in Country Music centers around the song, and ONE SONG ALONE can send your star soaring! Learn to create strong new songs, and you can be on your way to a fabulous career! The realness of today's country songs is a reason you may be able to create a HIT RECORD yourself.

In this book, you will discover the very best way to get that first job in music, how to move up in the business, and sell your songs. Better read this material carefully! Remember that you can start your plan of action as soon as you have finished reading this exciting book. If you act fast and promptly, I'll see to it at this end that this material of VALUE and proven practical usefulness will reach your mailbox QUICKLY! The price is only $12.00 plus $1.00 postage.

Musically Yours,

CREATIVE CONCEPTS

P.S. If your order is received here within the next TEN DAYS, I will personally send you a valuable BONUS REPORT that will be of extra SPECIAL use and value to you as you make your way upward in the glittering music field!

NAME (Please Print)_____
ADDRESS_____
CITY-STATE-ZIP CODE_____

SEND CHECK OR MONEY ORDER PAYABLE TO L. PERRY WILBUR.
Mail to: CREATIVE CONCEPTS, 814 Waterman Road South, Jacksonville, Florida 32207.

Mailing-List Brokers

On the following pages, you'll find some suggested mailing list brokers that will be helpful in the operation of your business. These list broker addresses are subject to change of address at any time. This list of mailing list brokers is reprinted with permission of *Opportunity* magazine. Please bear in mind that these addresses are subject to change.

Aaron's Names, 132 W. 24th St., New York, NY 10011
Mailing list; opportunity seekers zip-sorted on pressure-sensitive labels. Also multi-level names and other categories.

Ace Lists, 144 Nottingham Circle, Bridgeport, TX 76026
Mailing lists: multi-level buyers and opportunity seekers. Cheshire, peel-and-stick labels, magnetic tapes.

Ark. Investment Systems, 1530 Ivory, Horseshoe Bend, AR 72512
Names of financially established prospects. Zip-sorted, self-stick labels.

Brandon Communications, Dept. A, Drawer 5030, Monroe, LA 71211
Mailing list of opportunity seekers. Peel-and-stick labels in zip code order.

Computer Ad Mailing Lists, P. O. Box 17101, Ft. Mitchell, KY 41017-0101
Opportunity seekers and multi-level names on peel-and-stick labels.

Current List Productions, 776 E. Edison, Suite H, Manteca, CA 95336
Mailing lists of opportunity seekers. MLM and categories. Zip-sorted on pressure-sensitive labels.

Diante Enterprises, Inc., P. O. Box 70755-SO2, Chevy Chase, MD 20813-0755
Mailing lists printed on labels in zip sequence. Extra-income seekers, self-improvement seekers, do-it-yourselfers, weight-loss programs and more.

Group One Communications, (Norman Hill), Dept. 41A, P. O. Box 1539, Jensen Beach, FL 33457
Names available in hundreds of categories, for the small user or beginner as well as the volume mailer. Their lists are computerized on labels and guaranteed deliverable. Free details.

Informat Publications, Dept. 057-L, 4011 Valley View, Crystal Lake, IL 60014
Lists of mail-order buyers. Fully zip-coded on computerized peel-and-stick labels.

Leading Edge Mkt., Dept. B-3, P. O. Box 740329, Houston, TX 77274
Be a mailing list dealer; lowest wholesale prices.

Lelli Printing & Advertising, 2650 CR 175-05, Loudonville, OH 44842
Computerized names, zip-sorted on pressure-sensitive labels. Available: book buyers, opportunity seekers, multi-level, home workers, mail-order buyers, and small dealers.

Lincoln/Garza Enterprises, 3001-29th, Lubbock, TX 79410
Lists of mail-order buyers in most categories. Computerized, zip code order, peel-and-stick.

List Associates, P. O. Box 1033, Ames, IA 50010
Mailing lists of names, all available on peel-and-stick labels. Names are from publications such as National Enquirer, Field & Stream, and Popular Mechanics.

List Div., Box 316-SO, Irvington, NJ 07111
Mailing list: two million opportunity seekers.

Long Publishing, Dept. M14, P. O. Box 1465, Garden Grove, CA 92642-1465
Mailing lists of people who have inquired about Long Publishing business opportunity, or have bought books or other materials for financial enrichment. Peel-and-stick labels, 25¢ refund for any undeliverable.

LPM Associates, P. O. Box 133-OM37, Elmont, NY 11003
Mailing list for money-making or multi-level offers. Names are a maximum of 30 days old; computerized and zip-sorted on pressure-sensitive labels.

Mailmasters Int'l, Dept. 0-6, P. O. Box 704, JFK Int'l Airport, NY 11430
Get lots of mail. Receive free samples, opportunities, etc. One year $5.00.

McAfee & Co., 1-800-654-5541, in CA 1-800-654-5539, 589 San Gabriel, Manteca, CA 95336
Mail-order names—opportunity seekers. Zip-sorted pressure-sensitive labels. 22¢ refund for undeliverables.

Mid States, Dept. 0-2, 37847 N. Douglas, Lake Villa, IL 60048
Mailing lists of opportunity seekers, on pressure-sensitive labels in zip code orders.

National Junk Mail Director, P. O. Box 7777-V, New York, NY 10116
Send your name, address, and the statement "I am over 21" to this company and you will receive lots and lots of "junk mail." $1 requested.

New World Enterprises, P. O. Box 904, Monroeville, AL 36461
Names of opportunity seekers, computerized on peel-and-stick labels. All orders shipped UPS or first class. Same day service.

Promotions, 8050 S. Main, #2, Houston, TX 77025
Company will list you with hundreds of publishers, drop-shippers, firms wanting home workers, etc. For details send $1.00.

Quality Lists, Dept. SO-1, P. O. Box 1305, Seaford, NY 11783
Mailing lists of opportunity seekers and multi-level marketers. Gummed or peel-and-stick labels available.

Rainbow Trader, 350 S. Lake Ave., Suite 113-196, Pasadena, CA 91101
Opportunity seekers lists, in zip order on peel-and-stick labels.

Ready List, Suite R-262, 323 S. Franklin Bldg., Chicago, IL 60606-7069
Mailing list, peel-and-stick labels.

S. E. Ring Mailing Lists, Dept. B418, P. O. Box 15061, Ft. Lauderdale, Fl 33318
> Mailing lists—multi-level, opportunity seekers, mail-order buyers, gamblers, and more.

Seneca Valley Associates, Dept. 02, 131165 Shadyside Lane, Germantown, MD 20874
> Mailing lists of opportunity seekers, zip code sorted on pressure-sensitive labels.

Success Network, 10382 Park Ave., Suite B, Garden Grove, CA 92640
> Mailing lists of business opportunity seekers, buyers, and MLMs. Peel-and-stick labels.

Work At Home Programs, Inc., 781 W. Oakland Park Blvd., Suite 345, Ft. Lauderdale, FL 33311
> For a fee, your name and address will be sent to 300 companies that have work-at home offers.

P. O. Box 6638, Minneapolis, MN 55406 or phone 612-699-8918
> "Your flyers, promo sheets, coupons sent with other quality offers to any number of qualified prospects by first class mail for 3¢ each."

Philip E. Brancato, Sr., P. O. Box 237OP, Riverview, FL 33569
> Receive 1,000 names from successful salesperson's collection of customers. All on gum labels from any state. Write for additional information.

Cutters, Box 4359, Clearwater, FL 33518
> List of lottery and lotto dealers in the U.S. Pressure-sensitive labels. Zip-coded. Send for available states and listing.

Daley Wholesale, Box 113, Mohawk, NY 13407
> Names and addresses of Taiwan manufacturers. Deal direct and make a fortune. State kind of merchandise you are interested in. Receive a list of 100 manufacturers for only $4.95.

John Dreelin (Mailing List Consultant), 307 W. Kirkwood, Fairfield, LA 52556
> Mailing lists computerized in zip code order on peel-and-stick labels. Opportunity seekers and MLM.

Eddie Green, Jr., P. O. Box 36855, Shreveport, LA 71133-6855
> Mail order names. All categories on peel-and-stick labels. Fully computerized in zip code order. Receive details by sending SASE.

Income Sources Inc., Dept. C, P. O. Box 14474, St. Petersburg, FL 33733
> Buy mailing lists. Reproduce, rent, or sell to others. Just $35 per thousand for current opportunity seekers, multi-level names and

addresses. $5 extra per thousand for pressure-sensitive labels. Money-making bonus opportunity with first purchase.

Lake City Enterprises, Dept. 0-9, P. O. Box 72462, Salt Lake City, UT 84107
Proven buyer mailing lists computerized to meet your needs. Work only with names of actual mail-order buyers. Categories include: extra income seekers, self-improvement seekers, and work-at-home people. Free details.

Lelli Printing & Advertising, 2650 CR 175, Loudonville, OH 44842
Quality mailing lists are your road to success. Fresh computerized names, zip-coded for easy labeling and updated on a daily basis to assure you get quality eager prospects.

Mailing Lists, Dept. SO-10, 606 Merrick Rd., Lynbrook, NY 11563
Fresh, responsive and profitable mailing lists. Fully zip-coded on gummed or pressure-sensitive labels. Small and large test quantities arranged. Free details by writing.

Network Express 1-800-541-0900 (In California 1-800-334-3030)
Special category mailing lists: opportunity seekers, multi-level, mail-order product buyers from major magazines.

PLE-01, 2407 201st Ave., S.E., Issaquah, WA 98027
Responsive name lists of actual mail-order buyers. Most categories. Computerized in zip code order on peel-and-stick labels. Free details.

Pioneer, Dept. OPP11, Box 9070, Wichita, KS 67277
Fresh, computerized names on pressure-sensitive labels. Receive additional info by writing.

D. F. Scott Enterprises, Mail-Order Specialists, 1 Drury Lane, P. O. Box 1185(e), Waltham, MA 02254
Mail-order services—mailing lists, cooperative advertising, professional typesetting. Send a first class stamp to receive brochure.

Southlight, P. O. Box 3289, Oxford, AL 36203
Mailing lists of people who have bought $15 to $20 items. Gummed, computerized lists; five fresh names for every nondeliverable returned.

The Wayne Kelley Co., P. O. Drawer 389, Clanton, AL 35045
Names of opportunity seekers, zip sorted on peel-and-stick labels. 22¢ refund for undeliverables returned within 60 days of sale.

Paul C. Wilson, P. O. Box 1302-om, Valley Stream, NY 11582
Mailing lists of opportunity seekers. Maximum of 30 days old, computer printed on pressure-sensitive labels.

PCW, Box 1302-OM11, Valley Stream, NY 11582
Sell mailing lists. Send for free money-making business program.

S.M.I., Dept. 66, 1601 Main, Plainfield, IN 46168
Mailorder buyers available immediately. Thousands of mail-order buyers lists are now available for immediate use. Computerized on peel-and-stick labels in zip code order. Guaranteed deliverable. Write for complete details.

Saly's Sales Service, 709 Comer Dr., Clovis, NM 88101
Fresh, hot, responsive name lists of actual mail-order buyers. Most categories. Computerized in zip code order on peel-and-stick labels. Receive brochure by writing.

U. S. Business Services, 6910 Ludlow Building, Upper Darby, PA 19082
Free mailing lists. Limited time introductory offer exclusively for the readers of this publication. Fresh, Responsive. Active. Write for details.

W.O.E., 4863 Del Sol Rd., Colorado Springs, CO 80918
Hospital gift shop mailing list. Write for special one-time cost.

West 15 Company, 13175 Pageant Ave., S-101, San Diego, CA 92129
Mail-order names. All categories on peel-and-stick labels. Fully computerized in zip code order. People will respond to almost any bonafide mail-order offer. Send for details.

DataTech Communications, 148 So. Clayton St., Suite 106, Dept. 03, Lawrenceville, GA 30245
Wholesale name lists: computerized, self-stick, guaranteed. Multi-level, opportunity seekers, book buyers. Specify category.

Informat Publications, Dept. 016L, 4N270 Randall, St. Charles, IL 60174
Mailing lists. Fully zip-coded. Easy to use labels. Receive wholesale prices by writing.

Jodi Enterprises, 7141 N.W. 21st Ct., Suite 10, Sunrise, FL 33313
Opportunity seeker listings. Prime source for buyers. Receive details by writing.

Just Names, 11072 San Pablo Ave., Suite #2260M, El Cerrito, CA 94530
Mail-order names. All categories on peel-and-stick labels in zip code order. Guaranteed deliverable. Send SASE.

List-King Inc., 12 E. Walnut St., Kingston, PA 18704
Receive 5000 MLM names on peel-and-stick labels from any state, use of national toll free 800 number for one month, and free consultation. Lists are sold, not rented. $595.

Modern Everbest Products, P. O. Box 1089-H. Doylestown, PA 18910
Mail-order buyers and opportunity seekers mailing lists on adhesive labels. Receive prices by writing.

R & L, Dept. F6, Box 128, Circle Pines, MN 55014
Mailing list of opportunity/multi-level names. Receive prices by writing.

O. White and Associates, 10823 Sageriver, Houston, TX 77089
Mailing lists of actual mail-order buyers. Most categories. Computerized in zip coded order on peel-and-stick labels. Receive brochure by sending SASE.

PCW, Box 1302-OM10, Valley Stream, NY 11582
Receive money-making business program that tells how to profit in the mailing-list industry.

Some Final Hints

USING PEOPLE'S DOMINANT DESIRES

The reasons why people buy by mail can be traced to one or more of the dominant human desires. Customers will not hesitate to order by mail to fulfill their wants. A mail-order product or service that satisfies one or several of these wants will be sought after and bought, assuming the advertising for it is effective. These dominant desires of most people are

- To be healthy
- To save time
- To be clean
- To be popular
- To attract the opposite sex
- To make money
- To be praised
- To enjoy themselves

- To escape physical pain
- To satisfy one's appetite
- To keep possessions safe
- To save money
- To gratify curiosity
- To avoid trouble
- To be like others
- To protect their reputation
- To be an individual
- To be appreciated
- To have security
- To be in style
- To be secure in buying
- To be creative
- To have more leisure time
- To have influence over others
- To be successful
- To be important
- To take advantage of opportunities
- To be self-confident
- To avoid criticism

When you have a new product or service in mind for selling by mail-order, run down the above want-list and see if the item fulfills any of these desires. If so, how many?

Always remember, a mail-order product or service that fulfills a combination of these desires will have a lot going for it. Refer to this list for every new product or service item you consider launching.

OPTIMISM: YOUR GREATEST ASSET

Let me leave you with the following thoughts on optimism, which will be both your greatest need and greatest asset in selling.

OF ALL THE QUALITIES and traits needed for a successful selling career in this last part of the twentieth century, there's one that belongs at the top of the list. Practically every top-notch salesman or saleswoman has this valuable commodity in abundance. What is it? Quite simply, it is the spirit of optimism.

The spirit of optimism? It's around you everywhere! Super star Bob Hope has this wonderful spirit of optimism. He breathes and lives it. He has saturated his life, thoughts, and career with it. Bob Hope was born with the name of Leslie in London. He took the name Bob because he thought it sounds like a good fellow. His last name, however, is the magic of his name. "Hope" is an inspiring name to have.

Millions have only to see Bob Hope walk out on a stage and they immediately become happier and filled with more hope. Bob Hope has come to stand for more hope, a positive feeling, and a live spirit of optimism.

Anticipate Success

Why do you need this spirit of optimism in your selling? Because a salesperson — one who makes his or her living selling a product or service — must maintain optimistic enthusiasm to stay at his selling peak. With the spirit of optimism going for you, you won't fear calling on a big prospect you've been trying to land without success. You'll know that there's always hope that the prospect will become a customer or client.

Many sales are first made in the mind of the salesman or saleswoman. So the thoughts you think on any day in your career had better be positive, optimistic thoughts. Cliche or not, it's too often true that "if you can't make the sale first in your mind, you won't close it in real life."

Sales veterans with this spirit of optimism make themselves and the products they sell hard to resist. Why? Because this spirit of optimism is contagious. When you sound and act like your product or service is important to your prospect . . . and that you expect the prospect to do business with you, then you are definitely showing a spirit of optimism.

Don't Accept Defeat

When you feel confidence in yourself and in your selling abilities, you are also reflecting a spirit of optimism. Confidence? It rules the world. Turn back through the pages of history and you'll see confidence in action in the lives of most of the historical names of the past . . . the V.I.P. names. Alexander the Great had it. So did George Washington. Just a few of the many other names that come to mind include Winston Churchill, Victor Hugo, Jefferson, Ben Franklin, Eisenhower, Patton, give 'em hell Harry Truman, and Walt Disney. All of them had confidence in themselves, their abilities, and in life itself.

With the spirit of optimism strong in your mind and heart, you can face each day no matter what happens to you. If you hit a period of tough going and slow sales, you won't go into a tailspin. You'll know that your own faith in yourself, your product, and your company will see you through such periods. You'll know for certain that, in due course, you'll bounce back to more sales.

One of the major reasons England can look back on the dark days of World War II as its finest hour is because of the confident leadership of their leader — Winston Churchill. This great leader kept the confidence of the English people at a high peak. Even during the London Blitz, when the city was being bombed night after night, Churchill refused to abandon the spirit of optimism. He held to his belief that the tide would turn, as it finally did. Whenever you have a rough day or week in your selling, think about the courageous spirit of hope Churchill sparked in the hearts of the English people.

The truth is that if selling were never a challenge but always easy, it would bore many a fine salesman right out of the industry. If every sale you and your colleagues landed were an easy-as-apple-pie cinch, a lot of excellent sales veterans would start looking for the nearest exit door. A real salesman enjoys the give and take in selling. Half of the fun is the challenge, the game, the sense of meeting sales resistance and overcoming it. If you knew at the beginning of every sales presentation that you had the sale in the bag, most of what you know how to do best — *sell* — would seem to be wasted.

Knowledge Is Power

Selling will always seem like a hunt . . . an exciting game . . . to many who make their living in the industry. They believe in their products, their companies, and themselves. They usually know that the product or service they bring to a prospect will improve his or her life in some way or another. But the reason many of these pros are attracted to a selling career . . . and maintain a high production level . . . is the plain satisfaction of bagging the game . . . of closing the sale. Nothing else pleases them like making fresh new sales day after day.

We're not saying that all one needs for a successful selling career is a spirit of optimism. Other qualities are vital too. Judgment, good health and hard work are just a few that might be named. Applied in the selling field, with other right qualities, hard work can bring enormous profits. Judgment is the power to assimilate knowledge and the power to use it.

Have A Champion's Attitude

Wherever you stand today in your own selling career, remember that judgment can always be improved and industrious habits can be acquired. Even good health can often be attained or gained again. These qualities are the foundation of real success in just about any field and certainly in the selling arena. Added to what should be number one in your arsenal for success — the spirit of optimism — you can sell like a champion for a long time to come.

So remember. Where there's life, there is hope. And where there is continuing selling success of a high level, there is a spirit of definite optimism. Happy selling! ◄

A Recordkeeping Aid

The following chart will prove useful as your first orders come in.

Publication Ad Run in _____   Charge Per Word or Line _____

Address _____   Heading of Ad _____

Date Received	Name of Customer	Address of Customer	Amount Enclosed	Method of Payment	Date Order Filled	Key Code	Postage Cost

Bibliography

Alsop, Ronald and Bill Abrams. *The Wall Street Journal on Marketing*. Homewood, Ill.: Dow Jones-Irwin, 1986.

Bly, Robert W. *Secrets of a Freelance Writer*. New York: Dodd, Mead & Company, 1988.

Bonoma, Thomas V. *The Marketing Edge*. London: The Free Press, 1985.

Brumbaugh, J. Frank. *Mail-Order—Starting Up—Making It Pay*. Radnor, Penn.: Chilton Book Company, 1979.

Buxton, Edward and Susan Fulton. *New Business for Ad Agencies*. New York: Executive Communications, 1987.

Cohen, William A. *Building a Mail-Order Business*. New York: John Wiley & Sons, 1982.

Drucker, Peter F. *Innovation and Entrepreneurship*. New York: Harper and Row, 1985.

Goldstein, Arnold S. *Starting on a Shoestring*. New York: John Wiley & Sons, 1984.

Gosden, Freeman F. *Direct Marketing Success*. New York: John Wiley & Sons, 1985.

Harper, Rose. *Mailing List Strategies*. New York: McGraw-Hill, 1986.

Hogue, Cecil. *Mail-Order Moonlighting*. Berkeley, Cal.: Ten Speed Press, 1976.

Holtz, Herman. *How to Succeed as an Independent Consultant*. New York: John Wiley & Sons, 1983.

Horton, Thomas R. *What Works for Me*. New York: Random House, 1986.

Iglesia, Maria Elena De La. *The Catalogue of Catalogues*. New York: Random House, 1975.

Johnson, Wallace. *The Uncommon Man in American Business*. New York: The Devin-Adair Company, 1966.

Kishel, Gregory and Patricia Kishel. *Dollars on Your Doorstep*. New York: John Wiley & Sons, 1984.

Lewis, Herschell Gordon. *Direct Mail Copy That Sells*. Englewood Cliffs, N.J.: Prentice-Hall, 1984.

Lowry, Albert J. *How to Become Financially Successful by Owning Your Own Business*. New York: Simon and Schuster, 1981.

Ogilvy, David. *Ogilvy on Advertising*. New York: Crown Books, 1983.

Payne, Bruce. *Planning for Company Growth*. New York: McGraw-Hill, 1963.

Tilson, Ann and Carol Weiss, *The Mail-Order Food Guide*. New York: Simon and Schuster, 1977.

Wilbur, L. Perry. *Money in Your Mailbox*. New York: John Wiley & Sons, 1985.

Index

DATE DUE

~~MAY 1 0 1995~~			
~~OCT 2 6 1997~~			
~~APR 2 8 2000~~			

HIGHSMITH #45230

Printed in USA